The New Teacher's Complete Sourcebook

Grades K–4

BY BONNIE P. MURRAY

SCHOLASTIC
PROFESSIONALBOOKS

NEW YORK • TORONTO • LONDON • AUCKLAND • SYDNEY
MEXICO CITY • NEW DELHI • HONG KONG • BUENOS AIRES

This book is dedicated to...

————

...my mother, my first teacher

...the Wilsons and Dr. J., who taught me to learn

...Pat and Francie, who taught me to teach

...Karyn, who taught me to believe in my abilities

...and to all my students, children and adults alike,
who taught me to love

Cover design by James Sarfati
Interior design by Kathy Massaro
IIllustrations by Phyllis Harris
Cover photo by Vicky Kasala
Illustrations on pages 4-5 by Mike Moran
Photographs courtesy of the author

ISBN 0-439-30301-X
Copyright © 2002 by Bonnie P. Murray
All rights reserved. Published by Scholastic Inc.
Printed in the U.S.A.

11 12   40   09

Contents

Introduction

"**I** will survive!" declared Gloria Gaynor in her 1980s pop hit. But is survival enough? Wouldn't you rather *succeed*, especially in something as vital as your first year as a teacher? Years of educational research tells us that students rise to our expectations of them. So, too, do we as teachers rise (or sink!) to the expectations we hold for ourselves. Why accept second place when you can be the winner? Why just manage your students, when you can impact their lives? Why settle for survival when you truly *can* succeed as a first-year teacher?

Success doesn't come easily; it begins with a clear vision of what you want to achieve with your students. Then comes a great deal of work, and more work, and even more work! When you first begin teaching, the nights will be short, and what time you actually do have for sleeping will be spent dreaming of your students and your classroom. Effective new teachers breathe, eat, drink, and sleep their profession at first in order to build the foundation for a successful school year—and teaching career.

Although this may sound daunting, rest assured that you don't have to go through it alone. Just as Sleeping Beauty had a veritable army of fairy godmothers to ensure her success and happiness as a princess, so teachers need many mentors to guide them through the first year of teaching (and beyond!). In this guide, you will meet some mini-mentors who will share ideas to help you become a successful teacher. Let me introduce you to these resourceful, reflective, and reliable mentors.

Seymour Books is a book hound. He loves to share titles of great resources that will help you enrich your teaching experience. When you see Seymour, you can be confident that the book he suggests will be worthwhile.

Sir Chalott has dedicated himself to searching the Internet for great ideas. When Sir Chalott appears, head to your nearest computer and jump on the information superhighway for a free ride to great ideas.

Uneeda Halt is committed to making sure that you do the most important things first. She will pop up at times when you are no doubt thinking, "Sure this would be great to know, but I just don't have the time!" When Uneeda asks you to stop and think, remember "first things first," and give her your full attention!

As you make your way through your first years of teaching, I hope you will rely on them to help you find your way.

The New Teacher's Complete Sourcebook is designed to walk you through your first year of teaching with down-to-earth, easy-to-implement ideas and activities that promote success—for you and your students.

- **Part I** is a countdown of ten areas that need to be addressed before the first day of school so that you can blast off successfully into your career.

- **Part II** gives concrete ideas for handling that very important first day of school.

- **Part III** details the first month of school and what you can expect as students settle into their new classroom.

- **Part IV** discusses the remainder of the school year and describes numerous tools you might want to use to continually improve your teaching.

- **Part V** guides you through the end of the school year, helping you reflect on your first year of teaching and set goals for an even more successful second year.

This book focuses on the fundamental skills of teaching—planning, classroom management, instruction, and working with parents—rather than on methods for teaching literacy and mathematics. (I know you got plenty of those in your teacher education program!) These fundamental skills of teaching are essential for new teachers to develop. For example, no matter how well prepared you are to teach reading, you must first know how to manage your classroom to be successful. *The New Teacher's Complete Sourcebook* will assist you in developing and honing these necessary skills.

Now it's time for you to begin the countdown to the first day of school. As the immortal Dr. Seuss says, "Your mountain is waiting, so get on your way…" (*Oh, the Places You'll Go!*).

Pierre Tutor will direct you to a trusted peer at your school for site-specific information, mentoring, and peer coaching. Many of the questions you will have as a new teacher can only be answered with "It depends…." You must connect with at least one person at your school who can help answer all those "It depends…" questions. When Pierre comes along, be sure to find your flesh-and-blood peer tutor for the knowledge you need to succeed.

Mia First will continually encourage you to take time for yourself so that you can be a content, confident teacher. She recognizes the need for new teachers to take care of themselves throughout the year. When you see Mia, you may be tempted to ignore her, thinking that you're just too busy. But don't…when Mia is repeatedly ignored, she begins to fade away until there's no more "Mia," just work!

PART I

Countdown to a Successful Beginning

Welcome, teacher! You are embarking upon a career that gives you an unparalleled opportunity to make a difference in the world. Every day will be filled with surprises, new experiences, challenges, and excitement. While you may not see firsthand the love of learning that you have instilled in a child or the sense of responsibility that paves the way for a child to become successful in life, you have planted the seeds that will someday grow beyond your wildest dreams! As your students blossom into adults, you will live in their memories, and your influence will be passed on to people you will never meet, just like the ripples from a stone dropped in a pond. The habits of mind developed in your classroom will affect not only your students, but also their families, their friends, and eventually their coworkers. Your potential for changing the world is matchless. It's humbling, and perhaps a little overwhelming, when you realize that the future is indeed in your hands.

I would love to tell you that teaching is filled with golden moments day in and day out. I would enjoy describing the highs that arise from teaching. I would be thrilled to share a vision of perfection. But that won't do you any good. Yes, there will be many golden moments, feelings of exhilaration, and times when you approach perfection in the classroom. However, to achieve all this and more, a great deal of working and thinking has to come first. The opening section of this book is devoted to the hundreds of things teachers do before the first day of school to get ready for the grand adventure. It's time-consuming and occasionally tedious, but it's necessary. To teach well, you must prepare well. So roll up your sleeves and get ready to apply a great deal of "elbow grease" as the first day of school rapidly approaches!

A new teacher has so much to do! My first year of teaching was an endless stream of emergencies and urgencies, few of which I had anticipated. A friend of mine calls it "life on a banana peel." I remember panicking the day before school started when I overheard two experienced teachers discussing the parent letters they were sending out on the first day of school. I had never even thought of writing a parent letter, and I just couldn't imagine where I was going to find time in my jam-packed schedule to create one. I also hadn't planned for extra students who would register for school on the first morning of class and, therefore, weren't on my class roster yet; I didn't have enough chairs, desks, pencils, notebooks, or even smiles for the two extra children who suddenly popped into my classroom on the first day of school. After that first year, I made it a point to always be ready for the children who would register at the last minute.

It is inevitable that whatever you're not ready for will happen. My first day of teaching first grade brought a student birthday, a lost tooth, two scraped knees, and several tummyaches, as well as 28 little people with their individual needs, fears, joys, and parents! I left school that day (and many days to come) exhausted and scattered from all those unplanned experiences, and I promised myself that I would never again be unprepared. From that day on, I kept a list of the things I needed to do as they came up so that the next year I would be ready for anything. As luck would have it, I was moved to third grade the following year, which resulted in a whole new set of emergencies! Still, the list, with a few revisions here and there, has helped me get organized each year as I prepare for the first day of school. The new and improved "get ready, get set..." list has been broken into sections in this book to make it more manageable.

Now, it's time to get on with the countdown...!

What Bonnie didn't know is that there are several books of letters to parents already published, just waiting for teachers to adapt them. One of my favorites is *Educator's Lifetime Encyclopedia of Letters* by Susan and Steven Mamchak.

10...!

Define What You Expect of Yourself as a First-Year Teacher

Hey, wait a minute! I know you're thinking, "I don't have time for this... let me get on to the lists!" Well, listen carefully: *You will not truly succeed as a new teacher if you skip this step of the countdown!* So sit back down, read on, and get ready to dream—I need only about 30 minutes of your time right now, and the payoff will be great!

Let's begin the countdown with *your* vision of success. What does it mean to be successful in your first year of teaching? What does it look like, sound like, and feel like? How will you know you've achieved success?

As I mentioned in the introduction, expectations are highly predictive measures of what will actually happen. On days that I believe I'm confident and competent, I *am* confident and competent. On days that I believe I'm just another average person, I *am* just another average person. It's a constant mental exercise to create and nurture a vision that will plant your feet firmly on the path of success. Below is a brief description of the steps you need to take to achieve your vision. In the next few pages, you will explore each step in depth.

1 Dream.

If you are willing to settle for the ordinary, then this is not for you! When you dream, you identify what success as a first-year teacher really means to you. You commit yourself to the pursuit of that dream every day you teach, and you also assess how true you are to your dream.

2 Determine an action plan.

It takes time to figure out *how* to reach your dream. It is important to break the action plan into "baby steps"—small, manageable mini-goals—so that you continually progress.

3 Revisit your dream daily.

Once you have dreamed the dream, you must consciously strive to make it a part of your daily life. Tucking your dream away in some file folder won't help you remember it or achieve it. The workers at the Pike's Place World Famous Fish Market in Seattle, Washington (yes, there is such a place and, yes, it really is world famous!), post the company vision in their workplace, on their bathroom mirrors, on their refrigerators, on their car visors... anywhere they can see it and ponder it daily.

4 Measure and celebrate your progress.

When students are trying to master a new concept or skill, how can you determine their progress without regular assessment? The same is true of your vision. You should periodically check your progress and celebrate your success as a teacher along the way.

5 Identify and get help with roadblocks.

Even as you continually reflect on your dream and celebrate your baby steps, you will encounter barriers and hurdles to achieving your dream. Understanding these barriers will help you overcome them. The assistance of a trusted friend is often helpful in moving beyond the roadblocks.

Are you ready to dream? Let's get started.

Step 1: Dream.

Allow me to guide you through a simple visualization process to construct your dream. Read the following paragraph several times; then close your eyes and replicate the experience. Try to notice everything as you visualize your classroom.

Sit back and relax. Close your eyes. Imagine yourself entering the front door or gate to your school. Feel yourself walk through the halls of the school until you are standing outside of your very own classroom. Look around in your mind's eye and notice what you see as you reach for the handle of your door. Think about what you anticipate seeing, hearing, and feeling as you slowly open the door. Mentally take two steps inside your classroom. Move your eyes around the room counterclockwise, noticing the walls, floor, ceiling, furniture, materials…even the students. What are they doing, and what do you hear as they are working? What are students thinking and feeling in your classroom? How do you feel as you move further into the room and become a part of the scenario?

Now, try to recapture what you saw, heard, and felt in your mind's-eye. You may choose to draw, write, or do a little of both in order to represent what you noticed during the visualization exercise.

Dream a Successful School Year

☼ What will people *see* that indicates a successful first-year teacher when they visit your classroom?

☼ What will people *hear* that indicates a successful first-year teacher when they visit your classroom?

☼ What *feelings* will your classroom generate for you, your students, and visitors?

Summarize what it means to be a successful first-year teacher. Word it in a way that will inspire and guide you through your first year of teaching.

Step 2: Determine an action plan.

Wow! What a great dream! Now, how are you going to get there? An action plan will ensure that what you saw, heard, and felt during the visualization exercise will come to fruition. Reread your vision carefully. On the plan below, jot down two actions (use only 1A and 1B for now) that you can take to move forward with your vision. You will add to your action plan after you reach your first two goals (1A and 1B). CAUTION: "Become an expert at teaching reading" is too big of a chunk to bite off at one time! Use A and B to simplify your ideas into (two) smaller steps that will allow you to see progress quickly.

Have you seen the movie *What About Bob?* starring Bill Murray? Take a couple of hours and watch the video, paying close attention to the concept of baby steps. This will provide time for you to take care of yourself with a little laughter and work on your action plan at the same time!

My Dream in Action

I Will Achieve My Dream for Success by...

1A _____

1B _____

2A _____

2B _____

3A _____

3B _____

4A _____

4B _____

5A _____

5B _____

6A _____

6B _____

7A _____

7B _____

8A _____

8B _____

9A _____

9B _____

10A _____

10B _____

Step 3: Revisit your dream daily.

It's time to move on. You've envisioned what success looks like for you and posted your vision in several different places. You've begun to create an action plan to help you move toward your dream. Now, make a commitment to yourself to visit your vision and action plan every day for the next week. As you take the time to read and reread your vision, determine specific things you could do during the day to help your dream come true. Stay away from general ideas, such as "I'll be more organized today." Instead, be specific with thoughts, such as "I will pick up each piece of paper that comes across my desk only once today!" or "I will ask the custodian for three empty boxes today so I can sort materials." As you work during the day, periodically stop and ask yourself, "Is what I'm doing right now helping me reach my vision?" If the answer is "no," change what you're doing to align yourself with your vision. If the answer is "yes," give yourself a pat on the back!

Step 4: Measure and celebrate your progress toward the achievement of your dream.

Because it can be difficult to keep track of baby steps, I suggest that you designate a notebook as your "Celebration Journal." Place your vision and action plan in front. Then dedicate the rest of the book to weekly (or even daily) descriptions of the successes you've had as a new teacher. Keeping a journal can take just a few minutes of your day and will act as an anchor in times of stress.

◀ *This new teacher makes writing in her Celebration Journal a priority. As soon as the students leave each day, she takes time to reflect on the good things that have happened in the classroom.*

"I read this when things go wrong or just get too crazy, and it always brings me back to why I decided to be a teacher!"
　　　　　　　　　　　—Kathy Nartker

As you notice yourself making progress, bask in your success; then go back to your action plan and check off the items you have achieved. You might even want to write the date of each achievement. When you have checked off items 1A and 1B, go back to your vision and determine two more things you can do to continue moving in the right direction. Write these on 2A and 2B of your action plan. This cycle should continue all year long—looking back, noting successes, celebrating, and setting new goals.

Step 5: Identify and get help with roadblocks.

Teaching is a complex job with huge responsibilities right from the very first day. Many things can get in the way of your success as a new teacher. Some barriers may be generated internally ("I just can't do it!" or "I'm not doing anything right!") and some may be external (insufficient and/or inappropriate materials or supplies, an unsupportive staff, or not enough time in the day). It is critical that you talk with other educators when roadblocks appear on the horizon. A small roadblock can become insurmountable if you try to go it alone!

Numerous studies have been done on the ups and downs that teachers typically experience during their first year of teaching. The New Teacher Center in Santa Cruz, California, reports that the new-teacher cycle looks something like a roller-coaster ride. In working with new teachers over the last 13 years, I have seen this cycle in action as novices go through the highest highs and the lowest lows. The table on the next two pages describes the cycle and suggests some strategies to help you through each phase as you travel the new teacher roller coaster.

New teachers typically move through these phases during the first year— remember that you are not alone! ▶

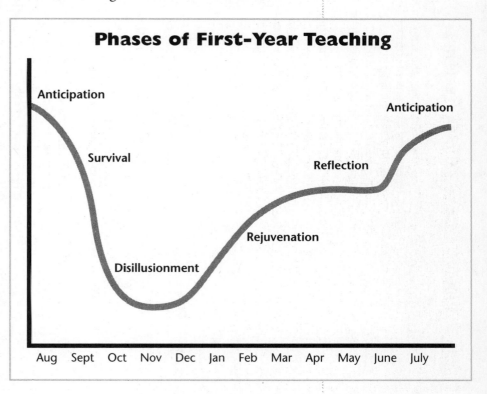

Phases of First-Year Teaching

Anticipation
Survival
Disillusionment
Rejuvenation
Reflection
Anticipation

Aug Sept Oct Nov Dec Jan Feb Mar Apr May June July

New Teacher Cycle

PHASE	CHARACTERISTICS	STRATEGIES FOR NEW TEACHERS
Anticipation	New teachers begin the school year full of excitement, certain that they are going to change the world. They have worked hard to earn a teaching credential and are ready to make a difference. They know that they will love all of their students and that all of their students will love them. They have a vision of the ideal teacher as the first day of school draws near.	☆ **Hold on to your vision** of what you expect teaching to be. The key is to learn how to teach without losing your excitement and idealism. ☆ **Begin building connections** with positive teachers at your site, at other schools, or online—when things become overwhelming, you will already have supportive relationships in place. ☆ **Keep a Celebration Journal** as described on page 12 so that you get into the habit of looking for the best in each day right from the start. ☆ **Start a notebook of "Ideas for Next Year."** All year long, make note of things you'd like to try or change, then revisit the notebook as you begin planning for next year.
Survival	The first month of school can be overwhelming. No matter how well prepared new teachers are, unexpected situations arise. They struggle with the day-to-day operations of the classroom and work countless hours each week. During this time, new teachers are on the hamster wheel, working as hard as they can, making it up as they go along, and running… until…they…finally…run…down.	☆ **Maintain your momentum** by reflecting on what is going well. Because you're so busy now, you may be tempted to set your Celebration Journal aside until you "get your head above the water." Don't! If you lose this good habit now, it will be nearly impossible to resume it when you need it the most. ☆ **Talk to other teachers** about specific ideas for lessons—why reinvent the wheel this year when others are willing to share the wisdom of their experiences? Use what others share THIS YEAR, and perfect it for yourself NEXT YEAR! ☆ **Forge a solid connection with at least one teaching peer** if you haven't already done so. Establish a sharing relationship and spend time together doing "teacher things."
Disillusionment	A combination of stress, exhaustion, illness, and overwhelming responsibilities can throw a new teacher right into the "pit of despair." The new teacher tends to focus on what hasn't been accomplished and what has gone wrong over the last several months. Report cards, parent-teacher conferences, and that dreaded first teacher	☆ **Take heart!** Getting through this phase will be one of the greatest challenges you face as a new teacher. Because it can last for approximately three months, you will need great persistence during this difficult time. ☆ **Reach out to friends and family** who may be feeling neglected. Let them know that while things are difficult right now, there is light at the end of the tunnel. Ask for their continued support and patience. ☆ **Reach out to your peers.** All that relationship building with peers at the beginning of the year will now result in support when you need it the most. ☆ **Ask for help,** or even just a shoulder to cry on. We've all been through this stage ourselves, so we'll understand!

evaluation are looming, bringing with them the realization that this is a never-ending job. Classroom management issues can be discouraging. Self-esteem may be at an all time low. During this phase, new teachers may begin to consider leaving the profession.

☼ **Visit other classrooms** and watch other teachers work with their students to gain lots of new ideas for managing your classroom. Another teacher may even be willing to come to your classroom and demonstrate a lesson or two. No matter how you go about connecting, just do it! New teachers who have a solid support network make it…those who don't, usually don't make it.

☼ **Keep journaling!** It is now more important than ever for you to find at least one good thing from every day. Remember that your teaching probably doesn't match your vision yet. It's okay. Success is a journey; give yourself time.

☼ **Continue to identify baby steps** that will lead you closer to your vision, and celebrate each achievement, no matter how small it may seem.

Rejuvenation

Teachers have survived the craziness of the holidays and had some time to relax with family and friends. They have made progress with classroom management and finally have time to do some planning and organizing for the rest of the school year. Spring is right around the corner, and the children are beginning to blossom right along with the flowers. It's apparent that the hard work is beginning to pay off!

☼ **Focus on curriculum development and teaching strategies** using your newfound confidence and energy.

☼ **Try something new** with your students and talk about the results with other teachers, even if it doesn't work out the way you had expected it to. Now that you have made it through the fire, you have valuable experience to share.

☼ **Expand your professional circle of peers** to include new and experienced teachers from other schools. Pooling ideas from multiple schools gives you many more resources.

☼ **Go back and examine your vision of successful teaching.** Bump up your action plan a notch.

Reflection

There's a rhythm to the class now and student learning is actually evident. It isn't as exhausting to plan, prepare, or teach, so creativity is starting to flow. New teachers are able to spend more time talking to veteran teachers. Now they begin refining their teaching, keeping what works, changing what doesn't, looking toward next year. "Reflection" leads to "Anticipation" for the new year, a new opportunity to grow.

☼ **Refer to your vision of the successful new teacher** as you begin to think ahead. Determine what you accomplished and where you need to continue refining your skills. Revise your vision if necessary.

☼ **Actively seek out partnerships with other teachers** as you begin to envision the possibilities that the next year holds. Select a teaching buddy who will plan with you and even observe and coach you during your quest for success.

☼ **Go through your Ideas for Next Year notebook** and pull out the best ideas. Set goals for next year and determine steps that will allow you to reach those goals.

☼ **Have a special celebration with your students**—you will never forget your first class!

"Why bring this cycle up now?" you may ask. "Isn't this one of those negative expectations that can drag teachers down?" I speak here as a former new teacher who barely made it past disillusionment. KNOWLEDGE IS POWER! I wish I had known that it was typical for new teachers to have feelings of fear, anxiety, and inadequacy when things wheeled out of control for me in October of my first year of teaching. If this knowledge had been shared with me, perhaps I would have been better prepared for the slump. Perhaps I would have remained more positive, knowing that there would be an upward trend if I could just hold on a little longer. More important, perhaps I would have reached out to other professionals for support rather than "toughing it out" on my own.

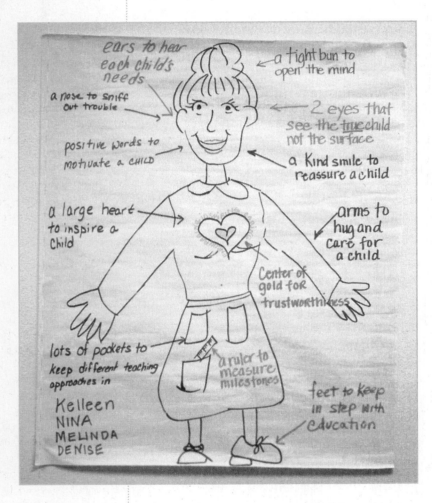

New teachers enter the profession with great expectations of themselves. Teachers who leave the profession during the first year typically do so because the reality of the classroom doesn't match their expectations.

Know Your State and District Expectations

To thoroughly prepare for the start of school, you must first seek out some information about your state and local school districts. There are countless policies, regulations, procedures, and information specific to your teaching location, which, if unknown, can have a variety of results, from mere embarrassment to an official reprimand to loss of your teaching license. The person at your school most likely to point you in the right direction is your administrator. Ask him or her for ideas on where to get the information you need. So, set aside an hour to put on your sleuth hat and start looking. The form on page 18 will help you organize what you learn as you investigate.

Learn About Your School

It is essential to grasp the intricacies of your particular school. Understanding the inner workings of your school will help you be more confident when you make decisions regarding management, planning, and instruction. When you receive confirmation of the school where you'll be teaching, you will need to investigate many issues to be well prepared. Ask questions of anyone at your site, but don't assume that whatever someone tells you is absolute, unless the person is the principal! Grab a fellow teacher, secretary, cafeteria worker, site administrator, and anyone else at your school who might have some answers. And do not worry about being a pest. Most educators love to share with those who love to learn. You'll probably need several hours to complete the questionnaire on pages 19–22. So, roll up your sleeves and dig in!

Tsk, tsk, tsk! I saw you start to turn to the next section before it was time. If you skip this section now, you probably won't return until it's too late! Think of it this way— would you be successful at Monopoly or Scrabble if you didn't take time to read the rules, hmmm?

Ahem! Don't forget that many states and school districts now have web sites that describe what drives education there. Pull up your web browser and type in the name of the school district or state. Click on the search button and see what appears.

Enhancing Professional Practice: A Framework for Teaching by Charlotte Danielson is an excellent resource, especially when state/ district teacher standards are missing or overly general. Danielson outlines 22 components of professional practice that have a direct impact on student learning. She also provides a rubric for each component whereby teachers may evaluate their performance. If you'd like to know how educators across the country define good teaching, check it out!

State and District Information
Scavenger Hunt

1 Has your state and/or district adopted or created standards for teacher performance? If so, where can you get a copy?

2 Has your state and/or district adopted or created standards for student achievement? If so, how are teachers held accountable for reaching the standards? For example, are the results of end-of-the-year tests reported to site administrators, the media, parents, or others?

3 Has your state and/or district adopted or created a teaching curriculum that must be followed? If so, where can you get a copy? If not, where can you get grade-level teacher's guides for subject-area textbooks?

4 What laws and regulations related to schools and classrooms are in force in your state? For example, what is your state's stance on corporal punishment, student privacy, special-needs students, suspicion of parental abuse or neglect, and so forth?

5 What are the district regulations and procedures in place regarding:

- flag salute and prayer or silence to begin the day
- student attendance and attendance records
- student discipline
- detaining students from lunch, recess, or special classes
- keeping students after school
- reporting to parents
- homework
- use of videos in the classroom
- use of the Internet in the classroom
- field trips

- holiday parties
- school emergencies
- inclement weather
- busing
- teacher and student dress code
- teacher workday hours
- teacher evaluation
- lesson plans
- grading and grade books
- sick days
- personal days
- substitute-teacher requests and preparation

6 What action must you take to get and maintain your teaching license/certificate? What are the deadlines for removing provisions like proficiency tests and additional course work to complete your license, and how do you go about removing the provisions? How and when must you accumulate professional development credits to renew your license/certificate?

The New Teacher's Complete Sourcebook: Grades K–4   Scholastic Professional Books

School Information
Scavenger Hunt

Who?

There are many important people to get to know at your school. Start by finding out the names and locations of the following folks:

☼ Administrators (principal, assistant/vice principal, other)

☼ Support Staff (office manager/secretary, clerk, nurse, custodian, cafeteria worker, instructional assistant/aide, campus monitor, other)

☼ Other Staff and Helpers (school psychologist, counselor, speech therapist, parent-organization leader, other)

☼ Teachers (teachers at your grade level, chairperson for your grade, teachers whose classrooms are nearby, art specialist, music specialist, PE specialist, library specialist, technology specialist, teachers for students with special needs and/or learning disabilities, teachers for the gifted or academically talented, teachers for English-language learners, other)

What?

Knowing your site guidelines, procedures, and expectations is a proactive way to step toward success. Below are some important questions to ask of site personnel:

Ask your principal...

☼ What are our school's vision, mission, beliefs, and goals?

☼ What are the school's guidelines for student discipline? If I have an emergency or chronic discipline situation, what procedure should I follow?

☼ How and when will I be evaluated? What will an evaluator expect to see and hear when visiting my classroom?

☼ How should my lesson plans look? What should they contain? Are there good examples available for review? How often will my plans be reviewed and when can I expect feedback?

☼ How are my long-range plans (if any) expected to look? What should they contain? Are there good examples I could see?

☼ When and how shall I prepare and post my schedule for instruction?

☼ When and how shall I get approval for parent letters?

(continued on next page)

School Information
Scavenger Hunt (continued)

☼ When and how shall I take and figure grades?

☼ What should my grade book look like? What should it contain?

☼ What are the guidelines for homework at my grade level?

☼ What are the guidelines and the schedule for teacher duty (if any)?

☼ Is there a mentoring program in place? If not, who would be a good teacher for me to talk to about school policies, classroom management, planning, and instruction?

☼ Other _____

Ask the office staff...

☼ What are the procedures for entering the school building when working after hours and on holidays or weekends?

☼ Where do I get audiovisual equipment (overhead projector, cassette player and headphones, TV/VCR, and so on)?

☼ When, where, and how do I get classroom supplies? What is available at the school? Do I have a budget?

☼ What are the procedures for taking lunch count and attendance?

☼ What is the procedure for sending students to the office? Do students need hall passes?

☼ What is the procedure for students who need to take medication or see the nurse? Is there a form I need to fill out when students are sick or injured?

☼ How do I arrange for a substitute teacher?

☼ Is there a class list available? Where can I locate my students' phone numbers and addresses?

☼ Which telephone may I use? How do I get an outside line? When and for what purposes is it appropriate for me to use the school phone?

☼ What is our school fax number? How do I use it?

☼ Is there a classroom aide or assistant who will be working with me?

☼ Other _____

(continued on next page)

The New Teacher's Complete Sourcebook: Grades K–4   Scholastic Professional Books

School Information
Scavenger Hunt (continued)

Ask your grade-level chairperson or other teacher...

☼ Does the entire grade-level staff do any planning together? If so, when will we start and what should I prepare?

☼ Does the school open for students and parents to visit the classrooms before the first day of school? Is there a parent orientation scheduled for my grade level?

☼ What schoolwide activities do we have (back-to-school night, open house, parent-teacher conferences, school carnival, science fair, holiday weeks, assemblies, student plays)? Is there anything I should be doing now to prepare for upcoming schoolwide activities?

☼ Where do I get resources and materials for teaching?

☼ Are there any special tricks I need to know when using the copier, laminator, or other machines?

☼ How do we take grades? Do we use portfolios or a traditional grading system? Where can I get a copy of our report card?

☼ Are there specific assessments and/or tests that we give at this grade level? If so, when do they occur and how do we typically prepare the students for the experience?

☼ What is the procedure for getting students to special classes (if any)?

☼ What are the procedures and rules for lunchtime?

☼ What are the procedures and rules for recess (if any)?

☼ What kind of behavior is expected of students in the hall and in common areas of the school?

☼ What is the procedure for restroom breaks? Do students need hall passes?

☼ What are the school guidelines for celebrating holidays and birthdays?

☼ What is the procedure for scheduling and preparing for field trips (if any)?

☼ What is the procedure for student buses (if any)?

☼ What are the procedures for emergencies (fire drill, missing child, student accidents, inclement weather, and so forth)?

☼ Other _____

(continued on next page)

School Information
Scavenger Hunt (continued)

Ask your custodian...

☼ Is there a handcart (dolly) for moving boxes and classroom furniture? Where can I find additional furniture OR get rid of excess furniture?_____

☼ How should the classroom look (chairs stacked, trash cans by doors, and so on) when the students leave at the end of the day?_____

When?

Knowing when things happen at your school is a great help for planning ahead. Find out when:

☼ Teacher day begins _____

☼ Teacher day ends _____

☼ Student day begins _____

☼ Student day ends _____

☼ Students are tardy if they arrive after _____

☼ Students are counted as being absent for half a day if they arrive after _____ or leave before _____

☼ Schoolwide morning routine (if any) _____

☼ Schoolwide closing routine (if any) _____

☼ Buses arrive (if any) _____

☼ Buses depart (if any) _____

☼ Teacher duty begins and ends (if any)_____

☼ Staff meetings are typically on (day) _____ at (time) _____ in (room) _____

☼ Schedule for inclement weather is _____

☼ Attendance must be taken and turned in by _____

☼ Lunch is at (if any) _____

☼ Recess is at (if any) _____

☼ Students go to special classes on (day) _____ at (time) _____ in (room) _____

☼ Specific students go to classes for additional support or teachers of students with special needs come to your classroom at _____

The New Teacher's Complete Sourcebook: Grades K–4 Scholastic Professional Books

7...!

Talk to Your Team Teacher and/or Teacher's Aide

While this section primarily focuses on team teaching, many of the ideas presented here also apply to working with a paraprofessional (teacher's aide/assistant). In either case, additional groundwork needs to be done before you can accomplish anything for your students. Entering a partnership with an attitude of making it work for the benefit of the students is essential. Anything that hinders a student's progress or negatively affects his or her well-being must be quickly and thoroughly remedied in a professional manner. You must first have a "meeting of the minds" where partners address expectations, responsibilities, and professional agreements. Being proactive by sitting down with your partner to establish some agreements for your team will minimize conflict.

One way to determine agreements is to use the List-Group-Label strategy (see page 146). Each partner individually lists ideas for "What I need in a partnership" or "What will make this an effective partnership" on index cards or sticky notes. Partners share their ideas, looking for common areas. These common areas become the team agreements.

> " The dominant principle of social life is not the struggle for existence, but cooperation.... If we would seek for one word that describes society better than any other, the word is *cooperation.* "
>
> —*Ashley Montagu*

By now, you may be feeling a bit overwhelmed with the volumes of information these questions generated. You're probably still thinking about all the things you need to do to get the physical space ready for the students and the short amount of time you have left to accomplish everything. Before you start to lose your cool, be sure to take a break and relax!

Stress Relievers:

◆ Phone a friend or family member and vent, or better yet, share something wonderful that has happened.

◆ Take a 15-minute walk to stretch your legs and reenergize your brain.

◆ Take a long bubble bath, complete with candles and relaxing music.

◆ Spend 15 minutes pulling weeds—it works wonders for frazzled nerves!

◆ If you're mechanically minded, take time to tinker with your car or your stereo, or even arrange your tools for future use.

◆ Play with your pet...or just watch its antics for a few precious moments of escape.

The team members also need to communicate their individual beliefs in terms of planning, classroom management, and instruction.

Beliefs and Philosophy—Educators tend to be passionate about strategies, techniques, and programs, which they adopt as a result of their philosophy of teaching. You and your partner will benefit from spending an hour sharing your perspective on the following questions:

◆ What things are so close to my heart that I can't give them up?

◆ What things, based upon my philosophy of teaching, do I disagree with?

◆ What are my strengths?

◆ What are my weaknesses?

◆ What type of classroom management program do I feel comfortable with?

◆ How do I prefer to assess and grade students in each subject area?

◆ How much extra time and money am I able to spend?

Planning—Decide how you will plan for instruction on a daily basis. Spend some time each day with both partners *present and contributing* to the planning process. Both partners must have a clear vision of what will be taught, who will teach it, how it will be taught, what materials will be used, how it will be evaluated, and what each partner will be doing during the lesson.

Managing—You will also need to arrange the classroom (see pages 39–48), determine your weekly schedule (see pages 98–100), and establish classroom procedures (see pages 75–77). It is important that you equally divide routine tasks, such as who writes the daily agenda on the board, who does lunchroom duty, who conducts the morning procedures, who collects homework, who cleans up at the end of the day, and so on. Tasks can remain consistent or be shared on a rotational basis—just make sure you and your partner know who is responsible for each task. Decide what you expect from students in terms of behavior. The following list was adapted from *Young Children in Action* (Hohmann, Banet, and Weikart):

◆ What rules are important?

◆ What student consequences, positive and negative, should be implemented?

◆ Should students clean off their desks before leaving the room?

◆ Should students raise their hands to speak, or may they speak out?

◆ Should students remain at their desks during work time?

- What noise level is acceptable to both partners?

- Should students be accompanied to the restroom?

- How will teachers get students' attention?

- Does everyone have to clean up just the things he or she used, or work until the whole room is cleaned?

- What will you do if a student is defiant?

- What if a student doesn't want to participate in a lesson? What if he or she is disrupting it?

Some things may change as the year continues, but all modifications should be agreed upon by both partners by evaluating the effectiveness of the teaming situation.

Teaching—As you learn more about each other's expectations, you can begin to explore effective ways to work together in the same classroom.

Keep in mind that your ultimate responsibility is to do what is best for the students—any challenge is worth the effort when the payoff is student achievement and well-being.

Find Out About Your Students

*N*ow it's time to learn more about the students who attend your school and, more specifically, who will be in your class. Having knowledge of the children you'll be teaching will help you make sound decisions about materials and resources, activities, the classroom environment, and classroom management techniques.

General School Population

*L*et's start by looking at the population of your school. Use the questions below to get a feel for the general population coming to your school this year.

⚙ **Is the neighborhood that your school serves new and developing or older and more stable?** *If you're teaching in a new neighborhood,* be prepared to have several students join your class during the course of the year as homes are constructed. This requires a great deal of flexibility on your part. It will be important for you to have on hand a number of "new student files," which contain information for parents typically given out at the beginning of the school year, assessments, welcome notes, and so on. (see page 61). It is also a great help to create a Big Book of classroom procedures to be shared with new students and to designate "buddies" who can introduce new students to the school and classroom. *If your school is in an older neighborhood,* get ready for parents who are very familiar with the school, administration, and other teachers. When I began my teaching career in an established neighborhood, a parent who had lived in the area for some time came to me before school started. I'll never forget the butterflies that attacked my stomach when she said, "Well, we know you're a new teacher, but we're going to give you a chance anyway." I quickly became very concerned about my status as a new teacher and realized that some parents were placing their children in my class under duress. There is a happy ending to this story—that parent became one of my greatest supporters. In fact, I recently saw her at the airport, and we had a wonderful time reminiscing about my first year of teaching.

Is the school populated with children who live in houses or apartments? Typically, a school surrounded by single-family homes is more stable. A school whose student population primarily comes from apartments may experience a high rate of transiency throughout the year. As with new neighborhoods that are growing, if you are working in an area of apartments, be prepared with a supply of "new student" folders and a Big Book of classroom procedures, as well as extra assessments, student supplies, desks, and chairs.

While new and growing neighborhoods cause you to gain new students during the year, with apartment neighborhoods you will most likely lose students as well. Be ready to fill out transfer paperwork and report cards throughout the year as students move away from your school. I found it helpful to send copies of assessments I had done on the transferred student with a narrative of academic and behavioral issues so his or her new teacher didn't have to start from scratch and waste precious learning time. Notice that I said to send *copies*—it is essential that you keep good records on all students, even those who leave your classroom midyear.

Do any homeless children attend your school? Know that if your school has a group of homeless children, transiency rates may be high as families move from area to area. Homeless children often lack school supplies for doing homework, so you may choose to put together a bag of school supplies for the child. You will want to alert public agencies that can provide backpacks, clothing, and even food for the children. I kept healthy snacks in my cabinet for times when homeless children came to school hungry. In addition, you may have a great deal of work to do in order to build trust with the children. Homeless students in my kindergarten class had a much more difficult time adjusting to a classroom setting than did my other students. Because the frequent changes in their lives kept them in a constant state of "fight or flight," the newness of kindergarten was overwhelming to them. I will never forget the look of panic on each of their faces when their parents or grandparents left the classroom for the first time. One child in particular completely shut down for the day, no matter how I tried to help him feel comfortable. It took about a week for him to even look at me, and weeks after that for him to engage with his classmates. In addition, any new experience, such as the first time going to the cafeteria for breakfast, was a major trauma for this homeless child. It took about a week of patient guidance to get him to negotiate the cafeteria on his own.

Another challenge was to facilitate relationships among my homeless children and the other students. Kindergartners are extraordinarily honest. They made no attempt to hide their unwillingness to work with children who were, in their words, "smelly." This was a truly heartbreaking situation for me as a teacher and it required a great deal of training on appreciating differences and being kind. Personal

My favorite children's book that deals with the issue of accepting others just as they are is *You Look Ridiculous Said the Rhinoceros to the Hippopotamus* by Bernard Waber. Another old favorite is *Crow Boy* by Taro Yashima. You might also want to share *People* by Peter Spier and *Whoever You Are* by Mem Fox for a look at likenesses and differences among cultures.

There are many Internet sites dedicated to working with the homeless. Try **www.naehcy.org/index .html** and **www.serve.org/nche**

hygiene was an issue that had to be handled immediately so that the rest of the students in the class would be more accepting of my homeless students. I asked local hotels for donations of soap and shampoo and actually had to teach some of the children how to wash. Much of the cleanup happened on a daily basis at school where there was running water.

For excellent information on working with families in poverty, I suggest *A Framework for Understanding Poverty* by Ruby K. Payne, Ph.D. This book will help you understand the culture of poverty and give you some very practical ideas on being successful in your communications with both adults and children.

What percentage of the students receive free or reduced lunch and/or breakfast? Many of the same issues for homeless students apply to low-income families. When I taught at a school that had about two-thirds of its students on free lunch, I was unprepared for how many families moved on a regular basis, depending on the apartment deals that were offered (for example, one month's free rent). As with homeless students, it was necessary to send home school supply packets and to structure homework so that it didn't require special supplies like glue or glitter. Also, be aware that families in poverty may use their school-age children to baby-sit younger siblings while the parent(s) are working two or more jobs. Be prepared to handle many student absences if this is the case. You may have difficulty reaching these parents by phone—some have beepers but no home phone.

Are students from other parts of town bused to your school? If so, you will need to find out about their backgrounds, in addition to those of the children from the neighborhood. Many magnet schools are placed in low-income neighborhoods and draw students from other parts of town in order to create integrated schools.

Did you know that the American *okay* sign (thumb and forefinger together in an "o" shape) may have a negative connotation for many people from Latin countries? For an inside look at some cultural no-no's, check out *Gestures: The Do's and Taboos of Body Language Around the World* by Roger Axtell and Mike Fornwald.

What ethnicities are represented within your school? What languages are spoken in the homes? The cultural makeup of your classroom will influence your planning and management. Once you find out what ethnicities will most likely appear in your classroom, you can do a little research. For example, in working with children of Latin descent, I learned very quickly that it was disrespectful for them to look an adult in the eyes when being reprimanded. Language differences or lack of parent literacy skills may also be an issue in working with a variety of ethnicities, so be creative about ways to communicate. I was fortunate to work in a school with a large bilingual staff, some of whom were always willing to help with translations and even sit in on parent-teacher conferences to facilitate two-way communication.

The Specific Kids in Your Class

At long last, we'll now take a close look at the children who will actually be in your class. Some of this information may not be available at your school right away. Be sure to note questions you will need to ask as the information comes in.

☼ **How many students are on your class list? How many are girls? How many are boys?** This information is essential for planning activities for the first week of school. A classroom that has a balance of girls and boys is a rare and wonderful thing! While the causes of differences in children are quite complex, certain characteristics tend to surface when a class is overloaded with one gender or the other. Often, a class predominantly made up of boys may be more independent and energetic and need frequent breaks and hands-on experiences as the students get back into the swing of things. A class mainly made up of girls may be more talkative and need plenty of opportunities to collaborate on projects, especially at the beginning of the school year.

☼ **Which students on your class list are new to the school?** This also creates differences in student interactions. A class full of students who have worked together in years past tends to exhibit a "class culture," depending on the group's prior experiences. Perhaps they have already established strong friendships, in which case "get to know you" activities will need to be structured so as not to be repetitious to the students. Perhaps they have been together for so long that they are highly competitive and even fractious—this situation requires an emphasis on trust-building activities when school starts up again. If your class list consists of several students who are new to the school, you will need to plan a school tour so everyone becomes familiar with the building, or even have a practice recess time to teach the playground rules. It will be helpful to know which students are new to the school, so you can assist them in connecting with other students who can "show them the ropes."

☼ **Which students on your class list have the same last name as their parents?** This sounds like a no-brainer, but many more children each year are being raised in blended families. I have been embarrassed several times in my teaching career, when I meet Johnny Smith's mother ("Hello, Mrs. Smith!") only to find out that she has remarried and is now "Mrs. Jones."

☼ **Which students on your class list are English-language learners?** If you know which students in your class are more likely to need assistance with the English language, you can start lining up

An exceptional book for fostering language development of English-language learners in English-only classrooms is *Amazing English*, available through Addison-Wesley. I refer to it continually, even when dealing with English-speaking students, due to its clear description of effective practices in balanced literacy.

translators, planning concrete learning experiences, and seeking additional help and materials to ease the students' transition into an English classroom. Check into policies and procedures for getting extra help for children who aren't in a bilingual classroom. The mother of my student from India helped her son to feel comfortable in his new classroom where he was immersed in English for the first time: She came to the classroom frequently where she was able to give her son one-on-one attention and the comfort of his native language while he was learning to be a kindergartner.

Which students require special services (special education, gifted and/or academically talented education, medication, disabilities/impairments, counseling or other emotional/ social/behavioral interventions)? All I can say is, "Forewarned is forearmed!" Find out who has special needs so you can be prepared for health- and behavior-related emergencies. For example, you should know which students have a history of seizures and what procedures to follow when a seizure occurs. Information about students with food allergies is essential for teachers who use cooking in the classroom or even those who enjoy planning pizza or ice cream parties for their students. It is equally important to know if one of your students tends to resort to violent behavior when feeling challenged. If such a student is placed in your classroom, you will want to request training on how to de-escalate emotional situations as well as how to handle a disruption.

Which students have siblings attending the same school? This is important in learning more about the families of your students because it helps you coordinate contact with the family. For example, during parent-teacher conferences, parents greatly appreciate having all of their children's conferences back-to-back on the same day, rather than scattered over several days.

To learn even more about your students from their parents' perspectives, copy the appropriate student information sheet on page 167 or 168 to send home on the first day of school. As the forms are returned to you, make note of any important information (food allergies, fears, attitudes, and so on) and place the forms in individual student files.

Envisioning Your First Class

In the next section, you will combine what you know about the general makeup of your school and the specifics of your actual class with child development theory to get the most complete picture of your students before school starts. As you review the following information about the characteristics of students at various grade levels, keep in mind that children are unique and that the information below only describes *typical* patterns of development. Look at the characteristics as a reference point for planning instruction and management systems that will most likely be effective for your grade level.

Learning about your students can involve a great deal of time, but it is time well spent and will help put you and your students at ease on the first day of school. Once you know enough about the children who will be joining your class, you can begin getting ready for them.

This is just an overview of child development. If you'd like to go more in depth, dust off those college textbooks! Or, to remind yourself that every child's developmental time clock is different, read *Leo the Late Bloomer*, a simple children's book by Robert Kraus.

Kindergarten (AGES 4–6)

One of the most challenging experiences of my career in education was teaching kindergarten. I was amazed at the huge variation in the skills and behavior of my students. At the beginning of the school year, kindergartners who are just turning five are very different from those who have been five for several months. In turn, five-and-a-half-year-olds are light-years away from kindergartners who are approaching their sixth birthday. Huge differences in behavior and skills exist depending on preschool experiences. With that in mind, if you are going to be teaching kindergarten, be prepared for anything! If you have never spent time in a kindergarten classroom at the beginning of the school year, you will be at a great disadvantage. I suggest that at the very least you devote several days to observing a pre-kindergarten class at the end of the year when they are getting ready to transition to kindergarten.

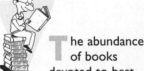

The abundance of books devoted to best practices in kindergarten speaks to how unique kindergartners are. One particularly excellent resource is *Positively Kindergarten: A Classroom-Proven, Theme-Based, Developmental Guide for the Kindergarten Teacher* by Beth Lamb and Phyllis Logsdon. If you are going to teach kindergarten, you must have this book!

Kindergarten
Observations and Implications

OBSERVATION	IMPLICATION
☼ Kindergartners are the center of their world.	Don't expect them to start school understanding how to treat others—you'll spend all year teaching this!
☼ They are oriented to their parents.	They may be frightened the first few days of school. Ask children who cling to parents to "baby-sit" a stuffed animal who is "a little nervous about the first day of school." Read *Owl Babies* by Martin Waddell.
☼ They learn by doing.	Incorporate play and other concrete, hands-on activities on a daily basis.
☼ They "drop out" when they lose.	Don't foster competition in games, work, or behavior.
☼ They believe in magic—what they see outweighs logic.	Enjoy this quality, but remember that it will affect their ability to understand mathematical concepts.
☼ They tend to be uncoordinated, even clumsy.	Have plenty of space between students during whole-group activities so they don't accidentally hit one another.
☼ They judge an act in terms of its reinforcement, whether it leads to punishment or reward.	Rewards and consequences are useful in helping kindergartners learn appropriate school behavior.
☼ They take pride in accomplishments.	Encourage and praise every child every day!

Teaching kindergarten is like herding marbles! If you have any doubt about that, watch the movie *Kindergarten Cop*. The process that Arnold Schwarzenegger goes through as he learns how to manage a kindergarten classroom is classic! You're probably ready for some time off, so watch and enjoy!

First Grade (AGES 5–7)

New first graders are really just veteran kindergartners! Unless their kindergarten program was full day, they tire easily, are constantly hungry, and often ask, "Is it time to go home?" After three to four weeks, they will have lost their kindergarten attitude and will be full-fledged first graders, ready to take on the world. The growth that you will see as a first-grade teacher is unmatched—enjoy every minute!

t's time to relax again! Hollywood gives a great example of the confidence that six-year-olds possess in *Home Alone*. In the movie, little Kevin deals with an overactive imagination, difficulty working productively with others, and an incredible amount of confidence. Treat yourself to an evening at the movies!

First-Grade Observations and Implications

OBSERVATION	IMPLICATION
☼ First graders are very literal in their interpretation of what is said to them.	Sarcasm is absolutely off-limits. Choose your words carefully so they aren't misinterpreted.
☼ They see the teacher as the source of all knowledge.	Again, be careful what you say. Direct children's questions of a moral or religious nature to parents so that you don't contradict parents.
☼ They enjoy group play.	Spend a great deal of time teaching them how to work productively in groups. Cooperative learning doesn't just happen for first graders—they have to practice cooperative skills and receive timely and specific feedback.
☼ They evaluate their own and others' behavior based on whether the act is considered "good" or "bad."	Read and discuss books about "appropriate" behavior. *No David* and *David Goes to School* (D. Shannon) are great fun. Carefully define rules for classroom behavior.
☼ They tattle on others.	Focus student attention on positives. For example, before going out to lunch, ask children to look for others who are being kind, responsible, helpful, and team players. After lunch (before the tattling begins!), ask children to tell the class about the children they saw doing the "right thing."
☼ They have a hard time making changes.	Have well-defined classroom procedures. Tell students ahead of time when you will be having a substitute teacher, and leave detailed descriptions of how things work in your classroom so there will be less need for change.

The opening scene of the movie *Miss Congeniality* shows a classic second grader with budding academic skills and a great spectrum of moods. Take a few minutes for yourself to watch and enjoy!

Second Grade (AGES 6–8)

Second graders tend to be calmer, quieter, and more organized than kindergartners and first graders. They have mastered a great number of academic skills and are ready to apply them in real situations—actually reading books of their own, using math in life. They may be serious, thoughtful, and sensitive, and can go from happy to sad in the blink of an eye. Relationships with other students become important, and even though "best friends" may "break up" after three days, these disruptions in relationships can be devastating for second graders.

Second-Grade Observations and Implications

OBSERVATION	IMPLICATION
☼ Second graders are capable of reflective thought.	When correction of behavior is necessary, ask them what happened, how it made them feel, and how they can fix it.
☼ They can sit quietly longer.	Don't abuse this—while they are capable of sitting, they still need to have opportunities for movement in and out of the classroom.
☼ They like to be in a group.	Peer pressure is a widely used motivator for second graders. They will work hard for the privilege of remaining in a group. If removed from the group for misbehavior, give them the opportunity to return as soon as they have reflected on why they were removed and what they can do to stay in the group next time.
☼ They can think in terms of classes, numbers, and relationships. Mathematical reasoning is becoming more logical.	While this is great for teaching math, it can cause problems for students who don't "fit in." Second graders judge harshly as they classify each other, and must be taught to appreciate differences.

Third Grade (AGES 7–9)

Third graders start the year with confidence. They are now in the same league as the "big kids." Third grade tends to be a "make it or break it" year. When I was teaching third grade and adults asked me what grade I taught, they would typically respond with "Oh, yes! I LOVED my third-grade teacher" or "Oh, yes! I HATED my third-grade teacher!" Third graders begin to build lifelong friendships and develop specific "favorites" and "dislikes" in terms of people, foods, music, sports, and school subjects.

When I watch *A Christmas Story* every holiday season, I believe the children in Miss Shield's class to be third graders. They are developing logic, lifelong friendships, and the skills to be successful students in the upper grades. Take some time out of your busy schedule for a little Christmas in July!

Third-Grade Observations and Implications

OBSERVATION	IMPLICATION
Third graders develop organized, logical thought. They are able to perform multiple classification tasks, order objects in a logical sequence, and understand conservation.	Science and math are exciting subjects in third grade. Children need to explore, ask questions, conduct investigations, and draw conclusions about a wide variety of topics.
They can converse at an adult level and communicate well.	While this is fun for a teacher ("They finally get my jokes!"), remember that they are still children and need to hear respectful language modeled.
They are dramatic.	Capitalize on their sense of drama by having them write scripts and produce plays for younger children. It will give them an outlet for acting, which may help minimize the drama provoked by relationships.
They assume responsibility for their actions.	Appreciate students when they "own up" to inappropriate behavior and actions. Help them learn to make positive choices.
They can now read and write with comfort and skill.	Expand their reading and writing to nonfiction so they can apply what has been learned.
They are confident in their abilities.	Let the students teach you and one another. Let them shine with all that they know and can do.
They look to the teacher as a model.	Build respectful relationships rather than trying to be their "buddy." Know that third graders are constantly watching you for cues on how they should act.

The boy in the movie *The Princess Bride* is very much like a fourth grader. The opening scene shows him playing a video game when his grandfather comes to read him a book. He is unmotivated and disinterested in much of the book until the action heats up. If you need a break, watch at least the first ten minutes to get a feel for the typical fourth grader!

Fourth Grade (AGES 8–10)

While third graders are confident and energetic, fourth graders go through a reversal stage where they lose confidence and become less expressive. They are almost completely oriented to their peers and will unite with them against outside forces. They seek independence from their parents, their teachers, and other influential adults as they look to their friends for approval. They begin to explore their feelings and become more understanding of why others behave and feel the way they do. They use language as a tool for socializing, learning, and influencing others. They want to know how things work and are able to analyze and think critically.

Fourth-Grade Observations and Implications

OBSERVATION	IMPLICATION
Fourth graders lack self-confidence.	Do not criticize them or allow them to criticize each other.
They relate more to the peer group than to adults.	Take advantage of their need to collaborate with peers through cooperative learning. Be aware that if you reprimand a fourth grader in front of his or her peers, the group will most likely unite behind the "wronged" student rather than behind the teacher.
They are interested in the outside world. Life no longer just consists of home and school.	Focus on social studies. Provide opportunities for field trips and guest speakers who can share their real-world experiences.
They are more independent and capable of self-direction.	Allow for choices in how they learn about topics and how they share what they have learned. Detailed and time-consuming projects are appropriate for individuals and small groups.
They experience a wide range of emotions.	Give daily opportunities for students to write about their feelings as well as to discuss their concerns in class meetings. Allow them time to deal with emotional issues.

5...!

Locate Resources for Teaching

Start at your school site to locate materials and supplies that are available to you through school funds. I used this giant "to find" list at the beginning of each school year; however, some of the items may not even apply to you in your situation. I listed all the supplies I could think of, but be aware that it is *not* essential for you to have them all the first day of school, and that your school may not be able to provide all of them for you. Acquire them in moderation and only if you really need them.

Classroom Resources: To Find...

— state/district curriculum, standards, and/or benchmarks (if any)
— teacher's handbook (if any)
— student's handbook (if any)
— instructional materials (literature sets, textbooks, teacher's manuals, supplements, manipulatives, maps, globes, computer programs and resources, and so on)
— informal reading inventory and other diagnostic materials for initial assessments (language, math, attitude)
— lesson-plan book
— grade book
— report cards
— attendance materials

— lunch-count materials
— hall passes
— tissues
— paper towels
— soap
— first-aid kit
— desk timer or bell
— flag
— copy paper
— transparency masters
— chalk or dry-erase markers, board erasers
— overhead markers
— stapler and staples
— paper clips
— thumbtacks
— straight pins and safety pins
— paper fasteners (brads)
— rubber bands
— teacher's scissors

— transparent tape and dispenser
— file folders and hanging files
— writing paper and/or journals
— drawing paper
— construction paper
— butcher paper, chart paper
— pencils
— glue
— student scissors
— rulers
— markers, crayons, or colored pencils
— single-hole and three-hole punch
— _____
— _____
— _____

Stop! Before you buy, check with other teachers at your school, your librarian, your university, and any new teacher support system your district or state may have. They may have activities, software, books, or magazines with ideas for teaching that you could borrow rather than buy. Once those resources have been exhausted, start bargain hunting! No matter where you go, let people know that you are a teacher. You will be amazed at the number of people who will give good deals to teachers!

Don't forget the Internet! One discount store that sells everything from student scissors to theme units is **www.classroomdirect .com**. Check it out!

Seek out freebies at:

◆ **www.rhlschool.com /free/freelinks.htm**

◆ **www.freestuffshop .com/teachers.htm**

◆ **www.freebie.com**

◆ **www.nea.org/grants /free.html**

The materials that are available at each school vary greatly. Once you have become familiar with the grade-level resources at your school, you may be interested in acquiring supplemental materials for your own classroom. If you decide to purchase books, math manipulatives, or other resources, spend with caution. Buy only those materials that can be used at a variety of levels, in case you move to another grade.

Discounted, Cheap, or Free

Check out these resources for great deals:

☼ **Garage sales** are wonderful resources for new teachers. You'll find books, puzzles, tapes, stuffed animals, decorations, and items you can use for math, science, and social studies.

☼ **Thrift stores** often have children's books and other neat things for your classroom at bargain prices. You may also be able to pick up an inexpensive camera to keep in your classroom for the wonderful times you want to record.

☼ **Public libraries** sometimes have more than a great selection of children's books. Many stock resources for teachers, such as theme units, book or tape sets, guides for using children's literature, and so forth. Some libraries also sell or give away old books or magazines that might be just right for your classroom.

☼ **Local bookstores** may offer a teacher discount on children's books. Call around to see who has the best deal.

☼ **Craft and material stores** may also give teachers a discount on items that teachers use in their classrooms, like felt, buttons, ribbon, fabric, and fabric glue. Before you buy, ask!

☼ **Ranger stations, visitor's centers, and other tourist centers** may be willing to give you materials for your classroom, or at least offer a teacher's discount. I had the good fortune to visit a local ranger station my first year of teaching. The ranger provided free bookmarks, fire-safety badges, posters, rulers, and pencils to give to my students.

☼ **Want ads** help you locate specific items that you need for your classroom. When I began teaching, I put a want ad for encyclopedias in the newspaper. Thanks to some kind folks who answered my ad, I received three encyclopedia sets, only one of which I had to pay for once the sellers found out that I would be using them in my classroom!

☼ **Book-order clubs** like Scholastic Book Club offer a wonderful selection of children's books at a discounted price. It's a great way to get books into your classroom library as well as into your students' homes. Book clubs also advertise discounted resources for teaching in their monthly mailers.

4ooo!

Prepare the Classroom Environment

Setting up the classroom entails the arrangement and organization of furniture, instructional materials, equipment, and supplies for safety and convenience. It also includes creating a warm, welcoming environment that will show students what an exciting and positive year it is going to be. Now it's time to take a tour through your classroom and prepare each component of the environment. As you work on your classroom, go back and take a look at your vision (see page 10). Make sure that the classroom's appearance is consistent with your dream of success.

The Door and/or Hall Outside of Your Classroom

Before the first day of school, you will want to post your name, room number, grade level, and the names of the students you are expecting in a prominent location, such as the classroom door. This welcomes the students to your class and lets them know they are in the right place. It can also set the tone for what to expect once students get inside the room. This first impression will be a lasting one for students, parents, administrators, and all who enter your room.

The "welcome" display may be as simple as "Ms. Murray's Second-Grade Stars," with student names written on large, colorful stars, or "Welcome to the Wonderful World of Third Grade," which uses cutouts of Earth for the student names. I always tried to make the welcome board theme-related so it could stay up all year. For example, if my theme for the year was interdependence, I might have used a large cutout of Earth surrounded by paper dolls holding hands, each doll with the name of a student in my class. I have also seen some adorable welcome decorations that stay up all year but are added to each month.

Students' pictures of themselves make intriguing decorations.

For example, place one teddy bear (or other cutout) on the board for each child, labeled with his or her name. In October, place mini-masks and trick-or-treat bags on the bears; in November, use pilgrim hats and feathers; in December, try Santa hats and reindeer antlers; and so on. Of course, be prepared to add names to the display as soon as new students register to join your classroom so they don't feel left out.

The Furniture

I gave my classroom the feel of openness, movement, and collaboration at the beginning of the school year by placing desks in teams around the perimeter of the room, leaving space for an open area in the front of the room for whole-group instruction. Spreading the desks or tables out allowed me to have easy access to all students. It helped to be able to reach every student by taking just a few steps in a semicircle rather than weaving in and out of closely placed desks or tables. Since I was rarely at my desk during instructional time, I preferred to place it in a corner of the classroom out of the way to allow more room for instructional activities. Keep in mind areas of high traffic when you are placing desks, storage carts, bookcases, and tables. Remember that the pencil sharpener, drinking fountain, and door should be easily accessible and that lunch boxes and backpacks should be kept out of the way. As the year progresses, you will have days when you just can't figure out why things aren't working. Try moving the furniture around; sometimes you and your students simply need a change! Some classroom arrangements are shown on the next page. You can decide which one would work best for you.

◀ *This classroom is ready—the only thing missing is a group of eager students!*

Classroom Floor Plans

KEY

Teacher's Desk With File Cabinet	Student Desk	Student Table	Center or Group Table

A

Bookcase · Wardrobe · Sink and Cabinet · Coat Rack · Chalkboard · Chalkboard · Bookcase · Bookcase · TV

B

Bookcase · Wardrobe · Sink and Cabinet · Coat Rack · Chalkboard · Chalkboard · Bookcase · Bookcase · TV

C

Bookcase · Wardrobe · Sink and Cabinet · Bookcase · Coat Rack · Bookcase · Chalkboard · Chalkboard · TV

Small-Classroom Tips and Tricks

Small classrooms are a real challenge to arrange. If you are teaching in a small room, you will need to find creative and effective ways to use the space you have. You may need to rethink and restructure the room layout frequently. When I walked into my kindergarten classroom for the first time, there was wall-to-wall furniture. I had half of a room and 27 children; there simply was not enough space to set up a proper kindergarten room, complete with areas for the necessary explorations. With a little ingenuity, I was able to orchestrate a workable classroom layout that met all my—and my students'—needs.

☼ **Remove excess furniture.** Instead of the large piano, I brought my small keyboard, which could be stored in a cabinet. Round and kidney-shaped tables were quickly "adopted" by other teachers who had more space. I kept only rectangular tables and a few desks in the room.

Thinking about how you want to teach will help you determine what classroom setup will work for you.

- ☼ **Store rarely used equipment out of the way.** I arranged for media equipment, which I didn't use on a daily basis, to be stored elsewhere. I did keep a student desk from which I removed the legs so that it sat six inches above the ground for a permanent listening center. The cassette player sat on top of the desk and the headphones were stored inside the desk.

- ☼ **Consider carefully your furniture needs.** Midway through the year, I decided my students did not need to have their own permanent desk or table. Eliminating just one table from the classroom and placing the other tables around the perimeter of the room opened up a large center area for whole-group activities, and provided space for centers, math manipulatives, reading and writing.

- ☼ **Explore creative management techniques.** Without the traditional seat-for-every-student arrangement, I struggled with how to engage the entire class productively. I finally hit upon splitting the class; half would work at the tables, and half would work in centers or on the floor. For example, while one half of the class was reading in pairs on the floor, the other half was working on journals at the tables. For some activities, I switched the groups, so that everyone could participate in both activities on the same day. For longer activities, I rotated the groups on different days, so that by the end of the week they had completed all the activities.

- ☼ **Create portable centers.** I was disappointed and frustrated that I didn't have room for permanent centers in my class. Then I discovered a rolling cubby unit with 32 tubs. I decided to make my centers portable by storing them individually in the tubs with a photograph and a written description of the center on the front of the tub. I included a two- by two-foot section of a heavy-duty plastic tablecloth in each tub. Students worked in pairs or alone on the floor and were restricted to their "center picnic" area as defined by the tablecloth. All center materials stayed in the tubs or on the tablecloths, so cleanup was a breeze.

This rolling unit made center storage and clean-up a snap! If you're short on space and no cubby unit is available, place center materials in plastic storage boxes or even copy-paper boxes, which can be stacked in a corner of the room when they are not in use.

Make use of every nook and cranny.

I stored math manipulatives separately from the centers by hanging clotheslines on the wall. I placed manipulatives in individual zipper bags (the bags with an actual zipper are much easier for children to open and close) and hung them from the clotheslines with clothespins. To help the children work on the floor without losing manipulatives, I made math mats out of 12- by 18-inch construction paper with two activity sheets laminated to each side. This helped keep the children focused on mathematical uses of the manipulatives.

There's always room for a clothesline. Just be prepared to teach your students how clothespins work, as they are a challenge for little fingers!

These kindergarten math mats had organizers for sorting, designing, counting, and geometric figures.

Set up an accessible library.

Because bookcases took up too much space in my small classroom, a friend suggested that I attach plastic rain gutters to the walls around the perimeter of the room for storing children's books. This allowed my kindergartners to find books more easily as the book covers faced out rather than the spines. It also spread my children out around the room when they were looking for books instead of creating a traffic jam around a bookcase.

It was easy to attach these plastic rain gutters to the wall. Please check with your principal and custodian first!

In choosing colors, ask last year's teachers for some general information about your students. For example, if your students are known to be active and chatty, you might select calming mauve as the main decorative color for your room, with a reading corner decorated in contemplative blue and a writing area in a background of calming purple.

Decorating your classroom can be very time-consuming. Remember these three words—*Progress Not Perfection!* Engrave them on your brain. Don't spend so much time on the walls and ceilings of your classroom that you run out of time for the really important stuff like preparing your management system, lesson plans, and getting ready to meet your students and their parents. Keep it simple!

Keep an Eye on the Senses

Much has been learned in recent years about the impact of visual stimuli on learning. In addition to organizing your classroom furniture for easy utility, don't hang excessive decorations—an over-stimulating environment makes it difficult to concentrate. Current theory on the brain's response to color suggests that teachers should carefully select no more than three main colors for their classrooms; more than that can be highly distracting for some children. Yellows and oranges tend to be energizing, while pinks, mauves, and purples are calming. Blues promote deep thinking and greens can enhance productivity. Reds are good for creative thinking and short-term high energy.

Many teachers pay special attention to the sensory atmosphere of the classroom. You may want to warm up your room by placing plants and table lamps near student reading and work areas. This creates a "just like home" feel. Music can also make a classroom environment more comfortable. Using music without words and without a driving beat will be less distracting for students. Nature sounds can be particularly relaxing and help focus children on their work.

The top of this three-dimensional tree was made out of a green sheet sponge painted with a few leaves. The trunk is brown butcher paper. The soft glow over this classroom library creates a calm mood and entices children to relax under the branches with a good book. ▶

Decking the Halls: Bulletin Boards and More

What about bulletin boards and room decorations? I was so thrilled to begin my career as a teacher that I spent a great deal of time and money on bulletin board decorations, only to realize that I hadn't left any room for the children to make their mark on the room. Remember that your room doesn't need to be decorated from floor to ceiling on the first day of school. Depending on your school's instructional programs, one of your bulletin boards may be dedicated to a math calendar, Mountain Math, or some other daily review program for math. That leaves one or maybe two bulletin boards to be decorated. I set aside a bulletin board to keep track of student progress on academic incentives, such as daily reading. On the first day of school, I had students decorate graphics to place on the bulletin board so that when we began the incentive, the tracking system was ready to use.

Another bulletin board or a portion of your classroom wall could be used to display student work. I prefer systems where *every* child's work is showcased rather than displays that are only for 100% papers. The teacher can select the student work or allow each student to choose his or her favorite piece of work from the week to display. Because you'll want to change the student work frequently, stapling papers to the wall is too time-consuming. I used large paper clips on the shoulders of child-shaped cutouts so student work could be easily posted and changed.

Students earned a sticker each time they returned their weekly reading contract. They used markers (not crayons) to decorate the incentive trackers so the stickers wouldn't fall off.

Aren't these silhouettes cute? I took pictures of the students on the first day of school and placed them on the appropriate boy or girl silhouette. The children were so proud to see their photos and their work displayed on the second day of school!

An "All About Me" bulletin board changes on a weekly basis. Begin the year by hanging pictures of you, your family, your friends, and your pets, as well as artifacts that represent your interests and neat things that you have done. Then, choose a different student each week to decorate the bulletin board with his or her own pictures and artifacts. This gives every student an opportunity to share something about himself or herself, as well as the responsibility of decorating a part of the room.

There is no shortage of books dedicated to creating useful bulletin boards. Browse through your university's or school's professional library, ask teachers at your school, or visit your local teacher's supply store.

Don't Forget the Ceiling

Having enough wall space in classrooms can be another challenge. Years ago, a teacher showed me a system of fishing line and clothespins hung from the ceiling; the clothespins make it a snap to hang and remove student work. I've hung a series of clotheslines across the ceiling for projects and decorations, or under bulletin boards for storage of bags of math manipulatives, writing materials, or other items that students need quick access to during the day. If you teach kindergarten or first grade, you will have to spend some time teaching children how to use the clothespins.

And don't discount the ceiling itself. Try placing instructional posters and learning aids there. In years past I've posted the following:

- word lists
- collections of synonyms
- alphabet charts
- information about how to write a friendly letter
- number lines

Children simply looked up when they needed to reference those materials.

Another wall space-saver is the whiteboard or chalkboard. Many are magnetized, and in addition to writing on them, you can use them for:

- agendas
- student attendance charts
- center rotation charts
- magnetic letter or number centers
- word walls

All you need is a roll of adhesive magnetic strips (available at craft or hobby stores) and a pair of scissors!

The Supplies, Materials, and Resources

Organizing materials and information is an art that cannot be easily taught because a person's organization system must take into account his or her style.

File It Away!

As a new teacher, you will need some kind of filing system—a filing cabinet or crates or boxes that have ledges for hanging files—prepared to store master forms you create, extra copies you run, information about each subject or theme, letters you send, letters you receive, test results, and other paperwork. When I began teaching, I occasionally made the mistake of giving my original of a story web or graphic organizer to a student, or misplacing it, so that the next time I needed it, I had to recreate it. I finally decided to make files for original forms that I use frequently (Reading,

Writing, Math, Incentives, Assessment, Planning, Parent Contact, Homework, and so on), and vowed to be faithful about filing all of my originals immediately after using them. When I found that I often had extras left over, I created a second file for "copies" to go with each "originals" file.

A place for everything… and everything in its place!

As I continued to build my files, I also needed a place for articles and ideas on each subject. I designated a third file "information" for each subject. I also made files for specific grade-level objectives. Placing information and originals for each objective and ideas for teaching it in files took only a few minutes, but greatly reduced the time I needed to prepare lessons the following year.

An excellent idea that a new teacher shared with me is to take several new file folders to every teacher training you attend. As packets and materials are distributed, simple label the folders and place the materials inside, ready to file when you return to school.

Store It

Before you know it, your room will fill up with supplies and teaching materials. Plan ahead to provide a space for them; see the box below for specific storage ideas.

Recently, I purchased several heavy-duty metal shelves and assembled them so there was room for two file crates on each shelf. Before I could afford shelving, though, I simply made a table skirt with butcher paper and a bulletin-board border to place around my work table. I stored several boxes under the table. This makeshift storage area hid a great deal of materials that would have otherwise been collecting dust.

To save time during class, I set aside an empty student desk near the front of the room to hold the day's instructional materials—if I left them on my desk, they were soon buried! A hint I received from a well-seasoned teacher was to keep an empty box handy for days when my desk was

Art Supplies and Math Manipulatives	○ baby formula cans or coffee cans (make sure there are no sharp aluminum edges) ○ peanut butter jars ○ sherbet containers ○ shoeboxes ○ plastic, zippered bags
Bulletin Board Materials	○ mirror and picture boxes from a moving company ○ two pieces of posterboard (laminated, if possible) stapled and taped on three sides make a large envelope for storing large, flat items. I made a giant envelope for each month of the year, as well as for each subject area.
Paper	○ plastic, stackable trays

overflowing—with one hand, I could scoop all the miscellaneous items into the box and slide it under my desk to be dealt with at a later time. Just don't let the box get too full or go too long without emptying it, or it becomes unmanageable.

Classroom Environment: To Do...

— prepare and pin up bulletin-board materials, calendar, alphabet, number lines, "welcome" sign, student work display board
— set up teacher's desk in a convenient but out-of-the-way location
— set aside a small table or desk for daily teaching materials
— set up student desks or tables with an eye to traffic patterns (grouping student desks allows for more open space in a room)
— set up mailboxes or crates, learning centers, class library, display tables, and group work areas, avoiding high-congestion areas
— set up a desk or work area for parent volunteers
— have Kleenex, pencil sharpener, and other high-demand supplies conveniently located
— get AV equipment and place near an outlet
— invest in "stackables" to keep different kinds of papers neatly organized and easily accessible
— prepare storage system for bulletin-board materials
— prepare storage system for arts and crafts materials and math manipulatives

— prepare files for:
  — substitute teacher
  — student information, work samples, and portfolios
  — grade-level objectives and theme units
  — holiday activities
  — helpful hints and ideas on teaching
  — teacher and parent correspondence
  — school bulletins and newsletters
  — test results
  — forms for reading, language, math, incentives, discipline, and parent contact

— _____
— _____

Send It Home

Remember to provide a place for student work and parent letters that need to go home. If you are on a tight budget, you can make mailboxes by drinking lots of milk and orange juice (or ask your neighbors to save their cartons for you)! Wash the cartons thoroughly, cut off the tops, and staple them together to make groups of 9 to 12 student mailboxes. Covering the groups of cartons with butcher paper or contact paper helps them last longer. My first year of teaching, I made three groups of mailboxes, so that I could place them around the room, eliminating the mad rush to one location at the end of the day. If space is an issue, use a plastic storage crate with ledges for hanging files. Place a file folder for each student in your class in the crate. This system makes it very easy to change from morning to afternoon kindergarten. All you have to do is switch crates, and you're ready to file notes home and student work for your next class.

3...!

Prepare Your Management System

Classroom management can be proactive—before issues arise—or reactive—after the fact. Establishing classroom rules and procedures are proactive measures that can prevent many misbehaviors from occurring. To provide a framework within which teachers can teach and students can learn, a teacher needs to have a consistent student self-responsibility program so that students know what is expected of them and what they may expect in return. I recommend that in preparing for the beginning of the school year, you determine which classroom procedures you plan to establish. Establishing rules is also important; however, since you will most likely establish rules *with* your students after school starts, I will discuss them in *Part II: Blast Off! Play by Play Through Your First Day*.

Establishing Procedures

In *The First Days of School*, Dr. Harry Wong says, "The number one problem in the classroom is not discipline; it is the lack of procedures and routines." Procedures differ from rules in that they are *expectations pertaining to specific activities and classroom routines* rather than guidelines for general behavior.

Establishing procedures in your classroom gives the students a consistent structure, frees up their memory for learning tasks, and saves you time and aggravation. When you were first learning to drive, you probably had to really focus when you were starting the car and putting it into gear; however, now that the procedure is automatic, you can probably think about other things while you perform it. Once students have internalized classroom procedures, you won't have to spend time telling them what to do each day. Procedures are also helpful on occasions when you are absent, as they allow the students to know what to expect and how to proceed; substitute teachers sometimes tell me, "I didn't even need to be in your class today. It ran itself!"

According to Dr. Wong, student success is directly linked to a well-managed classroom. Like rules, procedures are highly personal. Define what you expect of the students before school starts, but be flexible in case a procedure doesn't work for your class. You probably have a number of good ideas from your student teaching experience. In case you're looking for other ideas, below is a list of generic procedures; you'll need to adapt them to your grade level and school setting.

The *First Days of School* by Harry and Rosemary Wong devotes about 30 pages to the discussion of classroom procedures. For more information on how to establish procedures, get a copy—you will refer to it for many years to come!

General Classroom Procedures

☼ **Entering the room**—Enter quietly and politely; remove your hat if you're wearing one; don't interrupt other students; follow the appropriate procedure (morning, after lunch, after a special class).

☼ **Lining up**—Stand up quietly; push in your chair; take all necessary items; fold your arms; line up without touching others or talking; face the front of the line; watch where you are going.

☼ **Leaving the room**—Tell me where you are going; take the correct hall pass; do not run or play in the hallways or restrooms.

☼ **Beginning the day**—Enter the room politely; put away your backpack, lunch, and coat; turn in your homework; move your lunch clothespin (see page 52); sit at your desk and read alone silently.

☼ **Ending the day**—Clean off your desk; leave out your work notebook; pick up any trash within three feet of your desk; stack your chair; collect your mail; wait quietly to be dismissed.

☼ **Taking out/putting away/caring for supplies**—Share group supplies; recap markers and glue; check the number written on the supplies to make sure they belong in your group basket; if something belongs to another group, return it to them quietly.

☼ **Participating in group lessons**—Do not bring anything with you unless I ask you to; politely find a place to sit where you can do your best learning; sit flat, not on your knees; listen carefully for new information; raise your hand to speak; do not speak when someone else is speaking.

☼ **Obtaining help with assignments or social difficulties**—Quietly ask the students at your table if you need help with directions; if you are working alone, raise your hand to get help from me; if you are working with a group, ask them for help in understanding how to do the assignment; if you need help with social issues, write your problem in the "Problem-Solving Notebook" (see page 93).

☼ **Handing in finished work/homework**—Make sure your name is on your paper; place your paper upside down in the "finished work" or "homework" basket.

What to do with unfinished work—If I ask for work to be turned in, let me know when it isn't finished; if I ask you to keep an unfinished project, put it in your class-work notebook.

When and how to use the school restroom—If I am not teaching the whole group, stand by the classroom door with your hand raised; if I say "no," wait for a better class time to go; if I nod, leave the room quietly; do not play in the restroom; return to class before two minutes have passed.

When and how to use the drinking fountain or sink—When I am not teaching the whole group, you may get a drink; take only a three-second drink; you may bring a water bottle to keep on your desk; if you need to wash your hands, use only a little soap; wipe up any water you spill.

When and how to use the pencil sharpener—At the beginning of each assignment, the person I've chosen to be the "Pencil Sharpener" (see page 83) will invite you to have him or her sharpen your pencil; if your pencil breaks during an assignment, use a community pencil; only the Pencil Sharpener can run the sharpener and empty it.

Being a classroom helper; learning a classroom job—If you get a job on Monday, during silent reading time, see the person who did the job last week; ask him or her for the job description card and have him or her help you on the first day; for the rest of the week, it is your responsibility to remember to do your job (see page 82–83).

Getting into work groups—Take all the materials you will need; greet each other; complete the task doing your personal best; make sure each person signs the project; thank the others in your group.

Using the classroom library—When I am not teaching the whole group, you may check out a book; select a book—you only have three minutes at the class library; sign out the book on the sign-out sheet; take good care of the book; when you are finished, return the book to the basket and check it off the list.

Heading seat-work pages—As soon as you get a paper, print your first name and last initial at the top on the right-hand side and today's date at the top on the left-hand side.

Preparing for lunch—Wait quietly at your desk; when your lunch number is called, get your lunch or lunch money and line up in order; take everything with you, as you will not be allowed to come back to the classroom after we leave for lunch; while you're waiting in line think about the way you need to behave in the lunchroom and on the playground; while you're at lunch and at recess, find one person who is behaving responsibly and be prepared to tell the class what you noticed.

Talk to other teachers at your grade level as you develop your procedures. They can share procedures that are school-wide and give you ideas for the other procedures you need to establish. Once you finish defining your procedures, ask a trusted teacher to review them and offer feedback.

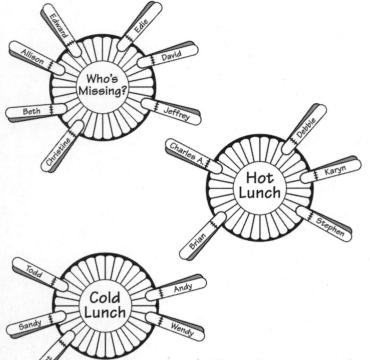

To make a quick and easy attendance/lunch count chart, simply staple three labeled paper plates to the wall—clipping the clothespins is much easier with the raised edges of the plates. If you have extra whiteboard space, take photographs of your students (or have them draw three-inch-tall self-portraits), attach a magnet strip, and stick them to the whiteboards. When students enter the classroom each day, they move their smiling faces to the correct column on the board.

☼ **Getting a tissue**—You may get a tissue from the closest of the four tissue boxes whenever you need one; you don't even have to ask; throw the used tissues away immediately; make sure it lands in the trash can; get right back to work.

☼ **Lunch count/attendance**—"Hot lunch" means you are having school lunch; "cold lunch" means you brought lunch from home or your parent is bringing it to you; first thing in the morning, move your attendance clothespin to the "hot lunch" or "cold lunch" sign; wait patiently for your turn; it helps to leave at least nine inches between yourself and the person who is in front of you while you're waiting.

☼ **Throwing away trash**—You may throw away trash whenever you need to, if I am not teaching the whole group; do not play basketball with your trash; make sure all trash lands in the can; pick up trash even if it isn't yours.

☼ **Turning in lost items**—Ask the people around you if they lost the item you found; if not, write your name and the date on a slip of paper and tape the item to it; if it is money or something valuable, put the item and slip on my desk for safekeeping; if not, put it in the Lost and Found box; give yourself a "pat on the back" for being honest.

☼ **Locating lost items**—Ask the people around you if they found the item you lost; if not, check the Lost and Found box; if it's not there, ask me at a time when I'm not teaching the class; if you find it, thank the person who turned it in; next time, try to take care of your things. *(NOTE: I go through the Lost and Found box at the end of each month with the whole class. If an item remains unclaimed, I give it to the person who turned it in.)*

☼ **Pledge**—When the "Flag Bearer" rings the "Liberty Bell" (see page 82), stop what you're doing and stand up immediately; place your right hand over your heart; say the Pledge of Allegiance respectfully; during the "30 seconds of silence," quietly think about the things you want to learn today and how you will act in class and on the playground.

☼ **Visitors in the classroom**—When visitors enter the room, let the "Host or Hostess" greet them (see page 82); when the Host or Hostess rings the chimes, get ready to listen to and look at the visitor—a smile is great!; when the Host or Hostess introduces the visitor, say, "Welcome to our class, _____"; remember, most visitors are here to watch you learn, so be ready to explain what you are working on in the class; treat visitors respectfully.

☼ **Fire drill**—Stop everything; stand up and head for the door quickly but without running or pushing; do not cover your ears; do not make any side trips; the "Fire Chief" takes the fire-drill packet and leads the line outside; the second person in line holds the classroom door for the rest of the class; the third person in line holds the outside door only for our class, then becomes the last person in line; wait patiently, calmly, and quietly in line outside until we are allowed to go back inside; walk back into the classroom calmly and get back to what you were doing.

☼ **Signals for attention**—When I need your attention, I will ring the chimes (or sound the rain stick, open the music box, and so forth); as soon as you hear the signal, stop what you are doing, look at me, and listen for directions.

I purchased my chimes from Books for Educators (1-253-630-6908). They are a lovely alternative to turning off the lights or raising my voice! ▶

☼ **Helping other students**—In a cooperative classroom, it is good to help one another; if someone needs help with directions or reading a word on an assignment, help him or her if you are able; if someone needs help with understanding the problem, tell him or her to ask me for help; never put down another student who asks for help.

☼ **Organizing desk**—Remove all loose papers; decide if they should go home or stay at school; put papers that should stay at school in the front pocket of your work notebook; put pencils or art supplies in your school box or shoe box; put your music folder, work notebook, writing notebook, theme folder, and reading book on the left side of your desk tray; everything else goes on the right side; pick up your trash.

☼ **What to do during free time**—If you finish an assignment, first work on any unfinished assignments that are in the front pocket of your work notebook; when you finish those, you may choose to do your classroom job, read a book, write a story, illustrate a book, make up math problems, work on a research project, peer-tutor someone who needs your help, or create a song about what the class is studying.

know this is time-consuming! Still, if you don't know how you want these classroom procedures handled, there will be confusion and misbehavior from day one. Now you need to write down your ideas for these very important procedures. Be thorough in creating and trying out your procedures to make sure they are complete and workable before you teach them to the students during the first week of school.

I know you still have so much to do to get ready for the first day of school, but you really shouldn't skip this section. Do take an hour or so to ponder these questions—you won't be sorry!

An Ounce of Prevention

◆ How will I dress on the first day of school?

◆ What will I do and say when I first meet my students?

◆ What will I do and say when individual students behave appropriately or inappropriately?

◆ What will I do and say when the class behaves appropriately or inappropriately?

Sit down with a copy of your school's report card, your district or state curriculum, your grade book, and a helpful teacher or two. Plan to spend about an hour collecting information about grading procedures from your peers.

Every Teacher's Guide to Classroom Management by Alice Terry has an idea for setting up grade books called the "One-Stop" Record System. It may be helpful for you to take a look at this system before starting from scratch.

First Impressions

Begin thinking about how you will encourage positive student behavior on the first day of school. How you look, what you do, and what you say will have a profound impact on the kind of relationship you build with your students as well as on their attitude and behavior.

The Dress Code

Did you know that within the first seven seconds of meeting someone, you make immediate (and difficult-to-dispel) judgments about that person? To create a good first impression with your students, you should be neat and clean on the first day of school, no matter how harried you might be with last-minute preparations. Let's talk about professional dress; what does that mean for a teacher? No doubt your school or district will have guidelines for appropriate dress. Consider that while a suit may be too formal for the first day of school, particularly in the primary grades, jeans and a T-shirt is much too casual. Be comfortable yet professional—you want students to be able to identify you as a teacher on the playground!

The Meet-and-Greet

What you do and say when you first meet your students sets the tone for the entire day, so take some time to think about how you will greet them. During your first day, you will no doubt have students who exhibit appropriate and inappropriate behavior. Have a plan for reinforcing individual behavior. See the chart on page 55 for ideas on greeting students and reinforcing their positive behavior.

Making the Grade

Now is the time to begin thinking about a system for grading. During the first month of school, you will want to fine-tune your grading system. At the moment, you need to find out what your school, district, and state expect in terms of recording grades so that you are able to meet these standards. For more specific information on assessment, see page 116.

Homework

Determine your expectations for homework—what it will entail, when and how it will be collected, and how it will be graded. Your school will most likely have guidelines for homework, so make sure you know what is expected. Are students supposed to have homework the first night of school? Find out and be ready with a meaningful assignment if the answer is "yes."

	GREETING STUDENTS	REINFORCING POSITIVE BEHAVIOR
Primary	○ Bend down to their level. ○ Shake their hands. ○ Say something positive ("I am so excited you are in my class!" "Wow! You can't possibly be a first grader! Are you sure you're not a second grader?" "I am so pleased to meet you!" "You really came prepared today!" "Look at how patiently you're waiting! Thank you!").	○ Be prepared with stickers, stars, and stamps to use as rewards, especially for kindergarten students. ○ Encourage individual and group behaviors with positive comments.
Intermediate	○ Respect their personal space; third graders don't usually mind shaking hands, but fourth graders may balk. ○ Don't gush. ○ Ask questions ("Were you at this school last year?" "Who was your teacher?" "Do you see any of your friends from last year?" "What is your favorite thing to do at recess?" "What is your favorite subject in school?" "What did you do that was fun this summer?").	○ Avoid reward systems that appear babyish or manipulative; see ideas on page 86. ○ Appeal to their sense of reason by offering them choices: "You may choose to continue what you're doing and complete the work during recess or you may choose to work now so you can be with your friends at recess. Which would you prefer?" ○ Reinforce group behavior and establish expectations by praising what the class does well: "Wow! You really know how to follow directions!"

Once you determine your homework policy, be ready to send that information home as soon as it is needed. A colleague of mine teaches her students (and their parents) to take homework very seriously. On the first day of school, the homework is for students and parents to determine an actual *location* for doing homework, a quiet place where the child can concentrate. The second day's homework focuses on gathering all the necessary *materials* to be successful with homework and placing it at the homework spot. Because this teacher takes the time to teach strategies for being successful with homework, she eliminates a great deal of confusion and lots of excuses like "The dog ate my homework" and "I couldn't find it!" Her students are very responsible in getting homework done correctly and turned in on time. For more on homework, see page 117.

An excellent resource, which you may have even picked up in one of your teacher preparation courses, is *Classroom Management for Elementary Teachers* by Evertson, Emmer, Clements, and Worsham. Your university library should have at least one copy available to check out.

Management Systems: To Plan...

— determine how you expect students to conduct classroom procedures
— prepare positive statements and actions for the first day of school
— prepare an individual and/or whole-group reward system
— determine your grading system
— plan homework for the first week of school

Prepare Lesson Plans and Materials for the First Week of School

*L*ooking at that blank new lesson-plan book can be intimidating. A great deal of work goes into planning for the first week of school, so it's a good idea to get started early. In-depth information regarding long-range planning, scheduling, and lesson planning is included on pages 94–103, but for now I'd like to refer you to pages 66–74 for specific activities you might wish to incorporate into your first day of school. In addition, the general things that you will most likely need during your first week of school are listed below.

Organizing That First Week

☼ **Setting up routines.** No matter what grade you teach, a large portion of your first week will be spent teaching classroom procedures (see page 75) and developing rules (see page 77). Allow plenty of time in your teaching schedule to explain, teach, practice, and reinforce all important procedures. Having so many procedures to learn can easily overwhelm students. *Be selective with the procedures you teach each day.* For instance, is it really necessary to teach the procedure for sharpening pencils the first day, or can you save it for another day by providing pre-sharpened pencils for your students? Do students need to know where they will turn in their homework, or can that procedure be taught on the first day homework is due?

☼ **Preparing for emergencies.** Recognize that you will need to take time to teach and practice emergency procedures. Many school districts have official fire drills within the first week of school to ensure that all students know what to do in case of fire.

☼ **Creating a non-threatening environment.** Pay special attention to designing activities that are low risk for the first week of school. Whole-group activities, such as Read Alouds before lunchtime, sharing information about yourself as a teacher, and practicing procedures, are all low risk. Small-group and individual activities can be low or high risk depending on the difficulty of the task, the way sharing is conducted, the expectations for the quality of work completed during the activity, and the time limitations for the activity.

☼ **Familiarizing students with school plan.** Take a tour of the school (or several mini-tours for younger students) and discuss school rules and procedures for common areas, such as the cafeteria and playground.

☼ **Keeping students engaged.** Be aware that after several weeks of vacation, your students may have difficulty getting back into the routine. Varying instructional activities frequently and allowing for "creativity breaks"—singing, miming, dancing, storytelling, building, drawing— will keep your students' minds engaged.

☼ **Planning a mix of activities.** Maintain a balance of individual assignments, paired activities, small-group collaborations, and whole-group lessons. *Whole-group* activities allow students to learn the rhythm of the classroom in a non-threatening way. *Small-group* activities help students get to know each other and let you observe interaction patterns. *Individual* activities give you an opportunity to learn more about individual students.

☼ **Assessing students informally.** You may begin assessing students after the first few days of school (see page 108). Make sure you don't begin formal assessments until the students are feeling comfortable with their new teacher.

☼ **Building community.** To create a classroom where all students feel comfortable, do at least one "get to know you" activity each day during that first week. This will help students connect with you and with their classmates, and it gets the class on the path to collaboration. I tried to balance social and academic activities during the first few days of school. I wanted my students to be happy at school and make new friends; however, I also wanted them to be challenged and excited about learning from the very first day of school. As you are planning your first few days' lesson plans, place yourself in your students' shoes—will they feel challenged, or like they played all day? Will they be interested or bored, happy to come back the next day, or fearful and stressed? If you're not sure that your lesson plans have balanced out, observe your students. You will soon see whether the activities have engaged, bored, or frustrated them. It's never too late to adapt and adjust instruction if what you have planned is not working!

☼ **Teaching!** And after all that, there still needs to be time for some serious instruction! I was heartbroken when a parent of one of my third graders said her son was disappointed on the first day of school because he "didn't really learn anything new." No matter how time-consuming laying the groundwork for a successful year is, make sure to challenge students and excite them about all they'll be learning in your class.

It's time to fire up your computer! I found some great ideas for the first few days of school at:

www.kinderkorner.com /back.html

www.kinderkorner.com/ back2.html

atozteacherstuff.com /tips/Back_to_School/

www.education-world .com/a_lesson/lesson019 .shtml

(also ...**lesson074.shtml** and ...**lesson073.shtml**)

Help students practice social skills in pairs during the first few days of school. When they become more comfortable, gradually increase group size to threes and fours.

Four Steps to Great Lessons

> We are continually faced by great opportunities brilliantly disguised as insoluble problems.
>
> *—Author unknown*

In preparing your actual lesson plans for the first week of school, I suggest a four-step process.

☼ **Step 1:** Write the schedule for your first week on a page, leaving spaces after each of the available times.

☼ **Step 2:** Examine the activities you have selected and estimate the amount of time you think each activity will need. Be as realistic as possible. Most teachers have a tendency to over-plan. Great! It is much better to have too much to do during the first few days of school than to run out of ideas at noon!

☼ **Step 3:** Place activities into appropriate spots on the weekly schedule, considering available time and ensuring a balance of fun and academics, individual work and group work, and sitting at desks and moving around.

☼ **Step 4:** Script out the plan for each day of the first week of school. In this script, you might choose to include ideas on how you will transition your students in and out of each activity, adaptations you will make for students with special needs, and how you will "shrink" or "stretch" the activity. While the best "sponge" activities are related to the actual lessons you are teaching, the following ideas may come in handy if beginning-of-the-year activities don't take as much time as you thought they would.

Sample Lesson Plan— Scripted Format

Grade: Kindergarten	Date: 9/5/00		**WG** = Whole Group	**SG** = Small Group	**I** = Individual	**P** = Partners

TIME	CONTENT	PROCEDURE	TRANSITION IN/OUT	ASSESSMENT	MATERIALS
12:45–1:10	Opening Language 9.2, 9.4, 9.6— Speaking: Social Studies 1.3— *See plan calendar objectives met on a daily basis	◆ **WG**—Have children hang backpacks, sing morning song, then come to circle and sit in spot ◆ **WG**—Monday and Tuesday, children's sharing ◆ **WG**—Singing:"Wonderful World," "Willie the Walrus," "Wings to Fly" ◆ **WG**—Go over today's agenda ("First, we will...") ◆ **WG**—Do pledge ("Stand up, raise right hand, put over heart, ready begin..."); sing "Grand Old Flag"; 30 seconds of silence ◆ **WG**—Do daily calendar with choral/physical responses	◆ **In**—Collect notes from home outside classroom; have children fold arms, tiptoe into room ◆ **Out**—Three clapping patterns		song charts and tapes, magnetic agenda pieces, "Grand Old Flag" tape, calendar and materials
1:10–1:30	Language 5.11—Letter names and sounds	◆ **WG**—Look at cover of *Mrs. Wishy Washy* Big Book ("Raise your hand if you can tell me something about the picture..."); book walk ◆ **WG**—Read Big Book aloud; reread with children ◆ **WG**—Introduce "w" (look at book; find "w"; ask, "What sound? what letter?"). ◆ **WG**—Look at "w" objects—walrus, wing, woodpecker, wig, wool, wood; make "w" sound; think of other things that start with "w."	◆ **In**—"Put on your story hat so you can listen..." ◆ **Out**— Simon Says		*Mrs. Wishy Washy* big walrus, wing, woodpecker, wig, wool, wood

Tried-and-True Sponge Activities

- When I say a number (day of the week, month…), tell what comes next (before).
- What number comes between 2 and 4 (13 and 15, 31 and 33, 49 and 51…)?
- Name (list) words that rhyme with ____.
- Name (draw, list) animals that live in the desert (jungle, farm, forest, mountains…).
- Name (draw, list) kinds of foods (dinosaurs, plants, holidays, cars…).
- Name (draw, list) things that are big (small, tall, short, wide…).
- Name (draw, list) all the colors you are wearing.
- Name (draw, list) things that are scratchy (smooth, soft, sharp, cold, sour, rough, fast, warm…).
- Name (draw, list) objects in the room that are the shape of a square (circle, triangle…).
- Use as many words as you can to describe the weather today (your friend, your teacher, your house…).
- Mime an animal.
- Find something in the room that starts with the letter "b" ("t," "c"…).
- Play hangman using the names of the students in the class.
- Play Simon Says.
- Do finger plays or sing favorite songs.

- List 39 ways to use a rubber band (piece of yarn, Kleenex, feather, paper clip, rock…).
- List all the foods you can think of that you like (don't like) to eat.
- List all the words you can make using the letters in your name.
- Draw a map of the furniture in your bedroom (living room, classroom…).
- List (name) one city (piece of clothing, type of food, animal…) that begins with each letter of the alphabet.
- List (name) synonyms (antonyms) for "nice" ("said," "bad," "mean," "pretty"…).
- Write (tell your elbow partner) what you would do if you found a dog ($100, a ring, a lost child…).
- Add the numbers of all the days of this month (all the numbers from 1–12, 1–100…).
- Alphabetize the names of the students in this class.
- List (name) all the words you can think of that end with the suffix "-y" (begin with the prefix "re-"…).
- Write advice for the President (actor, rock star, your grandma, your parents, your principal, your teacher…).
- Write (tell your elbow partner) "I feel happy (sad, angry, scared, excited, frustrated, curious…) when ____."
- Make a word search (scrambled words) with spelling words (theme words, holiday words…).
- Write clues about types of animals (foods, plants, the planets, your classmates…).
- Make up math problems for a friend to solve— make sure you can figure out the answer, too!

This is another good time to sit down with a fellow teacher and brainstorm possible responses and interventions for these first-day-of-school scenarios.

What will you do if...

◆ a child cries and runs after his mother?

◆ a child falls and hurts himself on the playground before school?

◆ an overly concerned parent will not leave the classroom?

◆ a child wets his pants?

◆ a child is hungry by 10 A.M.?

◆ three children answer to the same name as a joke when you call roll?

◆ you have more children than lesson materials?

◆ a child walks out of your class without permission?

Finishing Touches

O nce your plans for the first week of school are complete, begin gathering, creating, and copying the materials that you will need.

☼ **For you:** Place the materials for each day in folders labeled with the days of the week. I've also used large manila envelopes, small file boxes, or accordion files to hold materials that don't easily fit into folders. If you have set aside a table or desk to hold teaching materials and supplies, you will have everything readily available when and where you need it during that first busy, busy week!

☼ **For students:** In addition to preparing materials for specific lessons, other supplies will be necessary. Place a pre-sharpened pencil (kids are so anxious to sharpen their own new pencils that a great deal of time can be wasted) and a journal at each desk in preparation for the first day of school so children have something to work with immediately. You might want to put a community container with markers, glue, rulers, scissors, crayons, and other supplies at each group of desks. To keep from losing materials, consider using a permanent marker to label the contents of each container with the number of the team where the supplies belong. This enables students to return items that are found on the floor to the proper team with a minimum of fuss, and it gives the team responsibility for keeping track of each item.

Lesson Plans and Materials: To Prepare...

— prepare a schedule of daily subjects, lunch, special classes, and so on for your class

— place the agenda for each day where you and your students can easily see it (see page 128)

— write detailed lesson plans for the first week

— organize and set out teaching materials for the first week

— set up student desks with name tags, desk tags, *sharpened* pencils, crayons, glue, scissors, work folders, journals, and so forth.

— prepare for possible emergencies

— find out if you have duty the first day and/or week of school

Prepare to Meet Your Students and Their Parents

Before the Big Day

Be aware that some parents and students may come to meet you before the first day of school. Children are typically anxious to meet their teacher for the year, so allow a few extra minutes during your busy "setting-up days" for a special visitor or two. Some schools have a scheduled time for parents and children to visit the classroom and meet the teacher a day or two before school starts. Have your environment organized and be dressed like a professional, in spite of moving furniture! Be ready for younger students or siblings who want to explore the classroom—make sure that staplers, scissors, Exacto knives, and so forth, are put away. Also, if you don't want children playing with items, such as math manipulatives and center materials, have them stored out of reach until the first day of school.

To help your students feel welcome, call each child at home before school starts to introduce yourself and let him or her know that it is going to be a great year. This provides an excellent opportunity to chat briefly with the parents in order to begin creating a positive relationship with them. You may choose instead to send a "welcome" postcard to each child in your class; mail the cards a minimum of four days before school starts.

You will receive a class roster from the office before the first day of school. I always rewrote the class list in alphabetical order by *first* name (they're so much easier to remember than last names!), skipping lines to leave room to insert new students. I included students' names, phone numbers, birthdays, student ID numbers, parents' names, and any information regarding special needs (see page 166). This method of alphabetizing carried over into my grade book, mailboxes, and portfolios, as well as the seating arrangement for the first week or so of school to assist me in associating names with faces (seating was A–Z by first name, the A's closest to the door and the Z's farthest away). I also made name tags and desk tags for each student so I could call them by name whether they were in or out of their seat. After writing the names so many times, I found that I had practically memorized them before even meeting the students!

For my second year of teaching kindergarten, I decided to set up a welcome table outside my room with name tags and student information

> **"** *It is obvious that children will work harder and do things—even odd things like adding fractions—for people they love and trust.* **"**
>
> —*Nel Noddings*

Bonnie's first-day letter (page 63) covers a lot of information, but I suggest you look at samples of letters from teachers at your school for site-specific guidelines. When you finish writing your introductory letter, have someone else read it and make sure that the spelling is correct and that it makes sense. Then, have your principal fine-tune it (and approve it) before you send it home. Just a hint: Sign the letter before you copy it.

Little Rabbit's Loose Tooth by Lucy Bate is a fun book for little ones.

forms for the parents to fill out right there. I provided snacks and had my "parent packet" ready to give out so they had something to read after they left their "babies" at my door. This kept parents out of the room—they have a hard time leaving once you let them in the door! It also gave parents something to do while they were waiting for school to start.

If you are teaching kindergarten or first grade, or if you have a very large class, it's a good idea to enlist the help of another adult (NOT a parent from your class) for the day. This lesson was painfully learned on my very first day teaching kindergarten when I was literally beaten up by a scared five-year-old! I'm not kidding—the little guy decided he didn't want to be there, so he hit, kicked, and scratched me. Our intercoms weren't working at the time, so I had to walk the whole class to the office holding this wildcat in my arms to get assistance. Little ones need an amazing amount of attention. Having an extra pair of hands is a must, particularly when students are arriving and when they are being dismissed. No matter what grade you teach, getting your students to the right bus and to the right parents on the first few days of school is a challenge.

Have first-day letters prepared and copied so the students can share information about your classroom with their parents. I've included a sample welcome letter (see page 63) that gives specific information about the classroom. This is a good way to begin soliciting parent help in the classroom and to learn more about the students via the student information sheet (see pages 167–168), which can be attached to the welcome letter. Be aware of your parent population—your letter may need to be simplified or translated. The first day of school, I also sent out a discipline letter so parents wouldn't be surprised when discipline issues arose in class.

Missing Teeth, Birthdays, and Other Rites of Passage

Other helpful student preparations may include materials for lost teeth, birthdays, and other likely occurrences. If parties are not allowed for birthdays at your school, you may want your class to recognize the birthday child by writing a special note during writing time. The notes can be stapled into a birthday booklet and given to the child. Have students who lose a tooth write their name and the date the tooth was lost on a tooth shape to place in "Little Rabbit's Tooth Club." You could even use the tooth shapes to create a graph for math.

◄ *Losing teeth is a rite of passage in kindergarten through second grade.*

Sample Welcome Letter

August 26, 2002

Dear Parents,

Welcome to Room 17! I know that this will be a positive year for your child as we build on past successes and learn new things in third grade. With home and school working together, your child's academic and social skills will become even stronger throughout the year. Below is some important information about our class:

1. Our school hours are 9:00 a.m.–3:16 p.m. Students should line up and be picked up outside of our classroom.

2. Our lunch time is from 12:35–1:10 p.m. Your child may bring lunch or purchase school lunch, which costs $1.50. Please see the cafeteria worker for more information on various payment plans.

3. P.E. is on Thursdays and Fridays. Please see that your child is dressed for comfort and safety on those days (running shoes, comfortable clothes, shorts or pants for girls). We go to the library on Mondays (all library books must be returned weekly on Mondays), have music on Tuesdays, and do art on Thursdays (as art class can be messy, please have your child wear appropriate clothing).

4. Homework in my class will consist of daily reading, spelling, Family Math, and an occasional enrichment assignment. I will be explaining my homework, grading, and behavior policies in detail at Back to School Night on September 10, 2002. I hope you will be able to attend—I am looking forward to meeting you!

5. We will be taking many field trips this year. Please fill out the attached "Field Trip Permission" slip and return it *by Wednesday of this week* as we are going across the street from the school to do some nature observation activities Wednesday morning. I will keep your child's permission slip on file and will notify you of all field trips one week prior to taking them.

6. I will need several parent volunteers to help with field trips, to assist with my classroom writing and publishing program, and to make classroom materials. If you would be interested in helping in any way, please complete the parent helper slip below. I will contact you soon to set up a schedule.

7. I would like to learn more about your child from you. Please take a few minutes to fill out the attached "Student Information" sheet and return it to me as soon as possible.

8. This week I will begin taping your child's reading so we can have a good record of his or her progress throughout the year. If possible, please label and send in a blank cassette tape by Thursday of this week for the first taping. The tape will be returned to you at the end of the year.

9. Your child will need to bring a backpack or tote bag to carry to and from school daily and a school box or shoe box to keep in his or her desk. I have the necessary school supplies for groups of students to share, but you may wish to provide your child with his or her own personal colored pencils or markers, scissors, and glue. Please label items your child brings to school with his or her name. Please do not send toys to school as they are not allowed in the classroom.

10. Do not be alarmed if few worksheets come home to you. Much of your child's work will be kept in a portfolio for assessment purposes. You are welcome to visit any time to look through your child's portfolio, but please make sure to check in at the office to get a visitor's badge before coming to the classroom.

    I am looking forward to working with you and your child this year! If you have any questions or concerns, please contact me through the school office.

Sincerely,
Ms. Bonnie Murray

Parent's Name _____ Phone _____ Child's Name _____

— I would like to drive on one or more field trips.

— I would like to help with writing and publishing in the classroom.

— I would like to help with creating and/or assembling materials for the classroom.

Welcoming New Students

To be prepared for new students who join my class after the first day of school, I make five to ten "New Student" folders before school starts. Each time I send out an important parent letter, I make extra copies and place one in each folder. I also put a blank name tag, desk tag, mailbox tag, helper name card, sharpened pencil, journal, rest room pass, beginning of the year assessments, and an "I'm glad you're joining our class" note in each folder. When a new student arrives at my door, I simply pull out a "New Student" folder and have another student in the class assist me with introducing the new child to our class procedures.

Students and Parents: Get Ready...

— prepare class list/seating chart (alphabetically by first names helps)

— make name tags and desk tags

— prepare materials for birthdays, lost teeth, student of the week, weekly jobs, incentives, and so on.

— put student names on mailboxes

— prepare a welcome letter to send to each student before school starts, or to send home the first day of school

— prepare welcome letter and supply list

— prepare classroom rules and discipline policy

— make up student information form (see pages 167 and 168)

— gather school information

— prepare files and "first day" activities for unexpected new students; update these files with additional parent information throughout the year

— call or write each child before school starts to introduce yourself

— have a camera ready and loaded for the first day of school

— prepare something to distract nervous children (see page 66)

— arrange to have an extra person on hand for the first day of school

As you finish your last-minute preparations, take a deep breath and remind yourself of the vision you drafted earlier. You're on your way!

PART II

Blast Off!

Play by Play

Through Your

First Day

If you were fortunate to student-teach in the fall in the grade that you will be teaching, you probably have a very clear idea of what to do the first day of school. If not, thoughts of the first day may send shivers down your spine and butterflies into your stomach!

This section contains descriptions of what the first day might look like in an elementary classroom. Remember that these are just one person's ideas on how to structure the first day of school. I encourage you to adopt the parts that you think will work for you, but to impress your own style on your first-day plans.

First Day Schedules

A sample "first day of school" schedule for half-day kindergarten is given on page 75. The table starting on page 66 presents ideas for full-day kindergarten and first through fourth grades according to characteristics of the grade level. I have grouped the grades flexibly depending on the activity. For example, you'll notice that the plans for full-day kindergarten are separate from first grade at times and are combined with first grade at other times. These plans include about 280 minutes of instructional time apart from lunch and special classes like P.E., music, library, and art. The times indicated are approximate. Some groups of students will breeze through activities in no time, while others will need extra time. Flexibility is one of the greatest skills teachers can have during the first week of school— and beyond!

"The journey of a thousand miles starts with a single step."

—*Chinese proverb*

Sample First-Day-of-School Activities

Before the Students Arrive at School...

ALL GRADES

☆ If you have playground duty, make sure your door is locked and information on where the students in your class should line up is posted on the door. If you don't have duty, go outside at least 20 minutes before the morning bell rings, so you can greet your students and their parents.

Before School Starts...

FULL-DAY KINDERGARTEN AND FIRST GRADE

☆ Set up a "first day of school" table OUTSIDE of the classroom with name tags, student information sheets (bus stop, emergency phone number, and so on), and parent letters. You might also have parents note if their children are buying lunch at school or if they have brought their lunch. Parents can fill out the name tags and other paperwork while you meet students. Tell parents where and when their children will be dismissed.

☆ If young children seem nervous or ready to cry, try to distract them by finding an outgoing child from your class to show them the playground. If that doesn't work, get down on the child's level and ask him or her to "baby-sit" a stuffed animal who is "feeling shy" today, or to be your special helper for the morning. If that doesn't work either, have an extra adult (a friend, family member, or senior citizen, but NOT a parent from your class) on hand to "woo" the child.

SECOND, THIRD, AND FOURTH GRADE

☆ Greet your students individually. Introduce yourself to parents and tell them where and when students will be dismissed.

☆ Watch for students who seem extra nervous or shy. You can help ease the transition into a new class by chatting with them about their interests, books they like to read, subjects they like best in school, or what they did during the summer. You can also ask them to be your "assistant" for tasks like holding the door.

When the Bell Rings...

FULL-DAY KINDERGARTEN AND FIRST GRADE

10 minutes

☆ When the bell rings, instruct students to fold their arms and walk carefully inside. You will most likely have to show kindergartners what a "line" is—perhaps draw a line with sidewalk chalk and ask them to put a foot on each side of the line. Praise children who are following the procedure: "Wow! Alba really knows how to fold her arms."

☆ Leave the parents outside. If you let them follow their children into the classroom, they will want to stay! This is another useful time to have an extra adult available; he or she can ease parents' separation anxiety and escort them away from the classroom.

SECOND, THIRD, AND FOURTH GRADE

5 minutes

☆ When the bell rings, instruct students to fold their arms and walk inside respectfully. Model your expectations for what their line should look like and sound like in order to demonstrate respect for the other classes and teachers. If you talk in the hall, your students will too!

☆ Thank students who behave appropriately in line. If there is pushing or fighting, address it immediately before the class enters the school.

☆ Leave parents outside.

Opening Routines...

FULL-DAY KINDERGARTEN	FIRST GRADE	SECOND AND THIRD GRADE	FOURTH GRADE
30 minutes	*25 minutes*	*25 minutes*	*15 minutes*
☆ As students enter the room, lead them three or four at a time to hang up their backpacks and then sit on the carpeted area of the classroom. Teach them how to fold their legs when sitting on the floor.	☆ As students enter the room, have them find their desks (labeled with their names), hang their backpacks on their chairs, and sit down. Then teach the procedure for coming to the carpeted area, reinforcing positive behavior with specific comments.	☆ As students enter the room, have them find their desks (labeled with their names), hang their backpacks on their chairs, and sit down. Then teach the procedure for coming to the carpeted area. Thank children who are following the procedure.	☆ As students enter the room, have them find their desks (labeled with their names), hang their backpacks on their chairs, sit down, and put their name tags on. Be ready to get right to business as soon as everyone is situated.
☆ Express your excitement that the first day of school is finally here. Read *When You Go to Kindergarten* (Howe) to the class. As you look at each page of the book, ask "Who is excited about ____?"	☆ Express your excitement that the first day of school is finally here. Read *Froggy Goes to School* (London), *Franklin Goes to School* (Bourgeoise), or *My First Day of School* (Hallinan) to the students. Ask a few children to share their favorite part.	☆ Express your excitement that the first day of school is finally here. Read *The Teacher from the Black Lagoon* (Thaler), *Back to School for Rotten Ralph* (Gantos), or *Nobody's Mother Is in Second Grade* (Pulver). Ask a few children to share their favorite part.	☆ Express your excitement that the first day of school is finally here. Tell a brief story about something funny or cool that happened to you during your fourth-grade experience.
☆ Sing a song or two with the children. They may already know "The Itsy Bitsy Spider," "Five Little Ducks," or "Wheels on the Bus."	☆ Take attendance. Have your students' names prewritten on sentence strips and use them for daily attendance by asking a "yes/no" question, such as *Do you like pizza?* or *Do you want to be an artist when you grow up?* When you hold up a student's name, he or she answers the question (this helps you identify who can recognize their name in print). If a child goes by a shortened name or nickname, rewrite the name card immediately. Place the name on a pocket chart or	☆ To take attendance, call students' names and have them raise their hands to indicate that they are present. Ask them if the name you used is what they prefer to be called; many students go by a shortened name or nickname. Also, make sure your pronunciation is correct. Look each child in the eye and say, "I'm glad you're here today!" Give the students their name tags.	☆ Take attendance, calling students' names and having them raise their hands to indicate that they are present. Ask them if the name you used is what they prefer to be called; many students go by a shortened name or nickname. Also, make sure your pronunciation is correct. Thank each student personally for being on time and ready for class today.
☆ Take attendance. If you checked children in before school started, you can skip this step for today and save a little confusion. The first few weeks, call students' names and have them raise their hands to indicate that they are present. Look each child in the eye and say, "I'm glad you're here today!" Be aware that some students may not recognize their names or know what to do when you say them. After a few weeks, you can make name cards as			☆ Take lunch count. Teach children the correct vocabulary: hot lunch and cold lunch, school lunch and lunch from home. Have them stand up to be counted. Send the lunch count slip to the cafeteria. Tomorrow, you can

(continued)

Opening Routines... (continued)

FULL-DAY KINDERGARTEN	FIRST GRADE	SECOND AND THIRD GRADE	FOURTH GRADE
	described in the "First Grade" column.		begin using a system for attendance and lunch count like the one on page 52.
☆ Take lunch count unless you had the parents help with that before school. Teach children the correct vocabulary: hot lunch and cold lunch, school lunch and lunch from home. Have them stand up to be counted. Send the lunch-count slip to the cafeteria.	☆ graph and look each child in the eye and say, "I'm glad you're here today!" Now the class can count the responses in the "yes" and "no" columns.	☆ Take lunch count. Teach children the correct vocabulary: hot lunch and cold lunch, school lunch and lunch from home. Have them stand up to be counted. Send the lunch-count slip to the cafeteria. After a few days, introduce a system for attendance and lunch count like the one on page 52.	☆ Do the Pledge of Allegiance. Your students have been doing this for many years. Talk briefly about why schools take time every day to do the pledge. Ask a few students to share what the pledge means to them.
☆ Do the Pledge of Allegiance. This may be new for kindergartners, so model the proper stance with hand over heart and say the pledge. As the weeks go on, your students will start to say it with you.	☆ Take lunch count. Teach children the correct vocabulary: hot lunch and cold lunch, school lunch and lunch from home. Have them stand up to be counted. Don't forget to send the lunch-count slip to the cafeteria. In a few weeks, you can teach the students to use a system for attendance and lunch count like the one on page 52.	☆ Do the Pledge of Allegiance. Tell students that the flag stands for our country and all the good things that happen here. Remind them to be respectful during the pledge.	☆ Share your expectations for student behavior. Describe and model how you expect the students to ask questions or contribute to group discussions. Teach students your signal for attention. Explain that the students will be developing the actual rules for the class this week, and that for the time being, the expectations you have outlined will act as the rules.
☆ Share your expectations for student behavior. Say that kindergartners are all grown up now that they are in school. Describe what kinds of behavior you would expect from a "grown-up kindergartner." Describe and model how you expect the students to ask questions or contribute to group discussions. Teach students your signal for attention. Let students know that you will be looking for individuals who act like "grown-up kindergartners."	☆ Do the Pledge of Allegiance, modeling the appropriate stance.	☆ Share your expectations for student behavior. Describe and model how you expect the students to ask questions or contribute to group discussions. Teach students your signal for attention. Let students know that you will be looking for individuals who "do the right thing." Explain that the students will be developing the actual rules for the class this week, and that for the time being, the expectations you have outlined will act as the rules.	☆ Ask students for suggestions on the procedure they should use to come to the carpeted area of the classroom (e.g., stand up politely, push in your chair, walk to the front of the room, sit on the floor with your legs folded, show me you are listening). Have students join you in a circle on the floor.
	☆ Sing a flag song (the "Wee Sing Patriotic Songs" tape or CD may be helpful).		
	☆ Share your expectations for student behavior. Describe and model how you expect the students to ask questions or contribute to group discussions. Teach students your signal for attention. Let students know that you will be looking for individuals who "do the right thing."		

Learn Student Names...

FULL-DAY KINDERGARTEN	FIRST AND SECOND GRADE	THIRD AND FOURTH GRADE
5 minutes	**15 minutes**	**40 minutes**
☆ Tell children your name again. Create a rhyme with your name to help students remember it ("My teacher is Ms. Murray. She's always in a hurry").	☆ Tell children your name again. Tell them a few things about yourself. You could have a Big Book prepared with photographs of you, your family, and friends.	☆ Reintroduce yourself. Satisfy students' curiosity by talking about yourself. The first week of school some teachers decorate their "Student of the Week" bulletin board with information about themselves.
☆ Help students learn one another's names. Show them a microphone (a model of one is fine). Tell them that the only person who can talk is the one with the microphone. Take the microphone to each student so he or she can say, "My name is ____." The other students respond with, "His or her name is ____." There is something magical about a microphone—children love it!	☆ Help students learn one another's names. Sit in a large circle on the floor. Show them a beanbag and tell them that the only person who can talk is the one holding the beanbag. Pass the beanbag around so each student has a turn to say, "My name is ____. I like ____." Now go around the room again. Say "This is ____. Who remembers what he or she likes?" Then have the class repeat "____ likes ____." Introduce the song "What Is Your Name?" by Hap Palmer (*Learning Basic Skills Through Music, Vol. 1*). Palmer's web site has lyrics and activities: **www.happalmer.com/**.	☆ Help students learn one another's names. Brainstorm a list of positive adjectives as a class. Now have each student choose a *positive* adjective to describe himself or herself that begins with the same *sound* as his or her first name (e.g., Bright Bonnie). You can also play the "Name Game." The first student introduces himself or herself (name and adjective). The second person reintroduces the first, then introduces himself or herself, and so on. Students at the end of the game may need help to remember all the names and adjectives; make it clear that it is intelligent to ask for help. You should be the first and the last person to go.

Use Supplies for the First Time...

FULL-DAY KINDERGARTEN	FIRST AND SECOND GRADE	THIRD AND FOURTH GRADE
35 minutes	**35 minutes**	**25 minutes**
☆ Introduce the proper use and care of art materials. Instill a sense of pride in taking care of materials.	☆ Introduce the proper use and care of art materials. Instill a sense of pride in taking care of materials.	☆ Introduce the proper use and care of any art materials.
☆ Read *Mary Wore Her Red Dress and Henry Wore His Green Sneakers* (Peek) to the students. Ask students to describe what you are wearing. Model and think aloud how to draw a self-portrait. Ask students to go around the circle	☆ Read *The Important Book* (M. Wise Brown) to the students. Model and think aloud how to draw a self-portrait. Now add a sentence: "The most important thing about me is ____." Hang your self-portrait on the board.	☆ Have a few students at a time return to their desks. Reinforce appropriate behavior.
		☆ Have students create their own personalized desk tag on white

(continued)

Use Supplies for the First Time... (continued)

FULL-DAY KINDERGARTEN

and tell what they are wearing. Explain that they will make a self-portrait that shows what their hair looks like and what they're wearing. Dismiss children one at a time to find a place to sit.

☼ As they work on their self-portraits, help the students organize and label personal supplies at their desks. Then show them where they will be storing their backpacks, lunch boxes, and coats each day. Have a "sponge" activity prepared for students who finish early (see page 59). Demonstrate how you want the students to turn in their self-portraits and be sure to save them for assessment purposes.

☼ Involve all students in cleaning up. A cleanup song would be fun!

FIRST AND SECOND GRADE

Go around the circle and have students fill in the sentence "The most important thing about me is ___." Explain that they will be doing their own self-portrait and writing the most important thing about themselves. Dismiss children one at a time to their seats.

☼ As they work on their self-portraits, help the students organize and label personal supplies at their desks. Then show students where they will be storing their backpacks, lunch boxes, and coats each day. Have a "sponge" activity prepared for students who finish early (see page 59). Demonstrate how you want the students to turn in their self-portraits, and be sure to save them for assessment purposes.

☼ Involve all students in cleaning up.

THIRD AND FOURTH GRADE

8 1/2- by 2 3/4-inch card-stock strips. Show students a few creative examples and brainstorm other ideas before they start designing.

☼ Students who brought their own supplies may label them with a permanent marker and arrange them in their desks. Students who finish early can assist with taping the tags on the desks or choose a book from the class library. Show students where they will be storing their backpacks, lunch boxes, and coats each day.

☼ Involve all students in cleaning up.

Orient Students to the Classroom...

ALL GRADES

5 minutes

☼ Explain, model, and have a few students demonstrate procedures you've chosen to introduce today (see page 86). Continually model expected behaviors, prompt and practice desired behaviors repeatedly, and be consistent with positive reinforcement of desired behaviors.

Orient Students to the School...

FULL-DAY KINDERGARTEN AND FIRST GRADE

35 minutes

☼ Explain, model, and practice lining up at the door. Reinforce appropriate behavior.

☼ Give students a tour of the school.

SECOND, THIRD, AND FOURTH GRADE

25 minutes

☼ Explain, model, and practice lining up at the door. Reinforce appropriate behavior.

- Give students a tour of the school. Take the time to model, practice, and reinforce appropriate behavior and school rules. You might even have them locate where they will be sitting at lunch and go over lunchroom rules and procedures. If necessary, take a quick break outside to practice playground rules and procedures. Show students where they need to go during a fire drill; the fire department may conduct a drill during the first few days of school.

- If it is acceptable to lunchroom personnel, take a snack to the lunchroom so the students can have the experience of going through the lunch line, carrying food, sitting down, cleaning up, and practicing lunchroom rules.

- As the class leaves the lunchroom, take them by the restrooms and drinking fountains. Take a short restroom break, teaching and reinforcing appropriate behavior in the restrooms and in line. Show the children where they are allowed to play during recess and discuss the school playground rules. You might want to play a quick, organized game outside with the students to model correct behavior.

- Practice the procedure for fire drills and make sure all students know where to go and what to do during a fire drill.

Mathematics...

FULL-DAY KINDERGARTEN

40 minutes

- Introduce students to a few types of manipulatives you will be using in the classroom. Call them "tools" rather than "toys." Discuss, model (show examples of appropriate and inappropriate handling and use), and have the class practice using manipulatives during a few minutes of "exploration time." Review the signal for attention. Select a few students at a time to begin working with the manipulative sets at their tables. At the end of the exploration session, demonstrate and reinforce appropriate cleanup procedures, keeping in mind that "cleanup" may be a difficult concept for kindergartners and some first graders.

- Unless you have extra time, don't worry about beginning the math calendar or other daily math-review programs today.

FIRST AND SECOND GRADE

40 minutes

- Introduce the whole-class math calendar or other daily math-review program.

- Introduce students to a few types of manipulatives you will be using in the classroom. Call them "tools" rather than "toys." Discuss, model (show examples of appropriate and inappropriate handling and use), and have the class practice the correct use of manipulatives during a few minutes of "exploration time." Your role at this time is to observe and question children while they're working, as well as to redirect any students not following the procedures. At the end of the exploration session, demonstrate and reinforce appropriate cleanup procedures.

THIRD AND FOURTH GRADE

45 minutes

- Introduce the whole-class math calendar or other daily math-review program.

- Teach the students a "cool" math trick to get them excited about math at their new grade level. Marilyn Burns is an excellent resource for math games and tricks.

- Have students use manipulatives to figure out problems. I love to give each student a set of tangrams (you can make them out of tag board if there aren't plastic sets available) and read *Grandfather Tang's Story* (Tompert). In the story, as each animal morphs into another, I have students use tangrams to create their own version of the new animal. At the end of the activity, demonstrate and reinforce appropriate cleanup procedures.

Preparing for Lunch...

All Grades

15 minutes

☆ Give students three- by five-inch cards with their names, their student number (if any), your room number, and your name. For young children, use yarn to make the cards into necklaces so they don't lose them as easily. Make sure that students buying school lunch have their money, if they haven't already given it to the lunchroom. If young children can't hold onto their money during the walk to the lunchroom, carry it for them. Have cold-lunch students take their lunches to their seats. Line up according to lunchroom-personnel wishes. Take students to the lunchroom. You may consider eating with your students and joining them on the playground.

Language Arts...

Full-Day Kindergarten and First Grade

30 minutes

☆ Review the procedures for walking in a straight line and entering the room. Ask students to sit at their tables and lay their heads down while they relax to some calming music for 5 to 15 minutes.

☆ Review the procedure for coming to the floor area. Have a few students demonstrate.

☆ Take afternoon attendance.

☆ Read another book to the students, perhaps a Big Book so they can join in during the second reading. *Owl Babies* (Waddell) reminds young students that their mothers will return at the end of the day. *The Kissing Hand* (Penn) is another sweet book.

Second and Third Grade

30 minutes

☆ Review the procedures for lining up and entering the room. Ask students to sit on the floor when they come inside.

☆ Take afternoon attendance.

☆ Read to the students, either another first-day-of-school picture book or a chapter out of a book such as *Class Clown* (Hurwitz).

☆ Provide each student with a writing notebook. They can personalize the cover and set up a table of contents on the first 2 pages of the notebook, then number the next 20 pages. Have students write the date of the first draft on the top of the first page of each entry or story for reference. Insist that they never tear a page out of the notebook, as it is a working portfolio. Give them uninterrupted time to write (5 to 15 minutes to start with) on any subject they choose, with no focus on spelling or

Fourth Grade

30 minutes

☆ Review the procedures for lining up and entering the room. Ask students to sit at their desks when they come inside.

☆ Take afternoon attendance.

☆ Read a chapter of a book aloud. Choose a personal favorite, or try *Skinnybones* (Park) or *The Kid in the Red Jacket* (Park).

☆ Provide students with writing notebooks. They can personalize the cover and set up a table of contents on the first two pages of the notebook, then number the remaining pages. Have students write the date of the first draft on the top of the first page of each entry or story for reference. Insist that they never tear a page out of the notebook, as it is a working portfolio. Give them uninterrupted time to write (10 to 20 minutes to start with), on any subject they choose, with no focus on spelling or mechanics. After a few minutes share what you have written with the class during writing time. Demonstrate the use of your "Author's Chair." Model peer conferencing by asking the students if they can think of anything complimentary to say about your writing, then ask if they have any questions about what you wrote. Invite a few students to share their entries with the class.

✩ Have the students help you draw the characters from the story on a large piece of chart paper. Write the characters' names on the chart and have students help you draw arrows to the correct character. You could also have the students help you retell the story using a flannel board.

mechanics. Afterward, say that you'd like to share what you have written during writing time. Demonstrate the use of your "Author's Chair." Model peer conferencing by asking the students if they can think of anything complimentary to say about your writing, then ask if they have any questions about what you wrote. Invite a few students to share their entries with the class.

Content Area Instruction and Expectations...

FULL-DAY KINDERGARTEN

60 minutes

✩ Introduce students to the idea of learning centers. Discuss, model (show examples of appropriate and inappropriate handling and use), and have the class practice the correct use of center items. Review the signal for attention. Select a few students at a time to choose a center. At the end of center time, demonstrate and reinforce appropriate cleanup procedures.

✩ Allow time for an afternoon restroom break and recess when needed. Review the procedures and reinforce students for displaying appropriate behavior.

FIRST AND SECOND GRADE

60 minutes

✩ To get to know your students better, give each of them an outline of a picture of a treasure chest labeled "What I Want to Learn This Year," "Where I'd Like to Live," "What I Want to Be When I Grow Up," "What I Can Do Well," and so forth (see page 169). Fill in one of your own on the overhead. Students can share their completed treasure chests with several different partners so they can get to know a few of their peers better. The treasure chests can be placed on a bulletin board entitled "Discover the Treasures of Room ____." Have a plan for collecting the treasure chests.

✩ Introduce the first theme or unit of study. Have students brainstorm what they know or think they know about the theme or unit. Write their ideas on a piece of chart paper entitled "What We Know About ____." Now ask students to think of some questions or what they wonder about the theme/unit. Write their questions on a different piece of chart paper, to be explored later in the unit.

THIRD AND FOURTH GRADE

60 minutes

✩ To get to know your students better, have them make a "Me Bag." Give each student a paper bag and a magazine or two. Have them cut out pictures that represent their lives (hobbies, sports, favorites, family, pets, and so on) and glue them to the outside of the bag. Then have them find pictures of things that they don't like to put inside of the bag. Students can share their "Me Bags" with several different partners so they can get to know a few of their peers better. The bags can be placed on a bulletin board entitled "What's Your Bag?" Have a plan for collecting the bags.

✩ Explain the themes or units you have selected for the year. Introduce your rules for working cooperatively in groups, and then have groups brainstorm a list or web of things they know and would like to learn regarding the first unit. Have groups share their ideas. Keep the papers for future planning.

Prepare to Go Home...

Full-Day Kindergarten and First Grade

15 minutes

☆ Spend the last few minutes of the day with the students to review what was accomplished, what they liked, and what to expect for tomorrow. Have students draw a picture of what they liked best on the first day of school so that they have a paper to share with their parents. Give every child a sticker or stamp on his or her paper.

☆ Explain and model the procedure for cleaning the classroom. Reinforce appropriate behavior.

☆ Make sure every student receives a welcome and discipline letter to take home, along with any projects or papers from the first day. After a few days, you will introduce your mail system to the students; however, for today, just put each child's papers in his or her backpack instead of teaching the procedure now.

☆ Some students expect homework right away, so design an interesting activity for them to do when they get home.

☆ As students are waiting in line to be dismissed, ask them what they like best about their new school, new class, and/or new friends. Let the students know that you are looking forward to working with them tomorrow.

Second, Third, and Fourth Grade

15 minutes

☆ Explain and demonstrate the procedure for cleaning the classroom.

☆ Explain and model the procedure for picking up outgoing mail (see page 82).

☆ Make sure every student receives a welcome and discipline letter to take home.

☆ Intermediate students (and their parents) expect homework right away, so design an interesting activity for them to do when they get home.

☆ As students are waiting in line to be dismissed, review what was accomplished, what they liked, what was easy, and what to expect for tomorrow. Let them know that you are looking forward to working with them again tomorrow.

Dismiss...

All Grades

10–20 minutes after school

☆ When it is time to go, make sure your students know how to exit the building, where to wait for siblings or friends with whom they walk or ride, and where to go to catch their buses for home. This can be a stressful time for young children and students who are new to the school. Be patient as they will need extra help and attention from their new friend—YOU!

Half-day kindergarten has a flow of its own. Many of the activities will be done as described in the full-day kindergarten section, but over a period of days. See the full-day kindergarten plans for specific ideas to implement.

Positively *Kindergarten* by Lamb and Logsdon has great ideas for the first week of kindergarten. It recommends a graduated schedule for the first several days. It's worth looking into, especially for full-day kindergarten, which is a huge adjustment for little ones!

Sample Half-Day Kindergarten Schedule for the First Day of School

- ☼ (20–30 minutes before school) Meet students and parents outside

- ☼ (10 minutes) Enter classroom; sing songs or read a book

- ☼ (10 minutes) Take attendance; do the Pledge of Allegiance

- ☼ (5 minutes) Discuss expectations and rules for behavior

- ☼ (20 minutes) Read aloud; draw self-portraits

- ☼ (25 minutes) Restroom, drinking fountain, snack, and movement break

- ☼ (5 minutes) Quiet time

- ☼ (30 minutes) Mathematics

- ☼ (30 minutes) Learning centers

- ☼ (15 minutes) Prepare to go home

- ☼ (10 minutes) Dismiss students

Teaching Classroom Procedures

Before school started, you defined what you expect from your students in regard to rules, procedures, and work standards. But knowing what you expect is only the first step. You will need to spend plenty of time teaching each rule and procedure so every student in your class knows what the room should look like, sound like, and feel like.

Teach procedures as the need for them arises, starting with essentials— restroom use, using the sink, getting a tissue, throwing away trash, and getting the teacher's attention. Have individual students demonstrate the

> " *T*o be a teacher is painful, continual and difficult, and it is to be done by kindness, by waiting, by warning, by precept, by praise, but above all, by example. "
>
> —*John Ruskin*

proper way to do various tasks in the classroom, such as lining up, then ask the class if they can do it the same way. It may seem like wasted time, but a 15-second student demonstration of how to line up correctly each day can save you hours of transition time and frustration all year long. Here's an example of what I might say when teaching students about my procedure for lining up:

> *Ladies and gentlemen, it's almost time for us to go to P.E. Since this is the first time we'll be lining up as a class, let's talk about the appropriate way to line up. What are some things that you know about lining up?* (students answer) *Great ideas! I think we should line up just as you suggested—stand up, push in your chair so no one trips over it, fold your arms so you aren't tempted to touch anyone or anything, and line up without talking so the rest of the school can continue to work while we're in the hall. Is there anyone in this room who can demonstrate the procedure for lining up? Thanks, Susan! Go ahead. Notice how Susan remembered to push in her chair. Wow! Her arms are folded and she's not even talking to anyone or touching anyone on her way to the line. Terrific! Who else can demonstrate? Is there a whole team that is ready?*

Students will occasionally need reminders of how you expect them to do things. I like to post the main procedures, such as starting the day, ending the day, using the class library, using the restroom, and so on, in appropriate places in the room so students can easily refer to them. I also have my students create a Big Book of procedures entitled "How to Do Things in Room 17." I list one procedure per 12- by 18-inch piece of white construction

I f you didn't student-teach at the beginning of a school year, it may be enlightening to watch one of your peers establish and teach procedures. If you can't get to another teacher's classroom during the day to observe, ask if you can set up a video camera to record him or her teaching procedures. It helps to follow the observation or taping with a quick conference to discuss what you noticed. Please obtain your administrator's approval before videotaping a peer's class.

To ensure that every student remembers your classroom procedures, create a Big Book or individual charts describing each procedure.

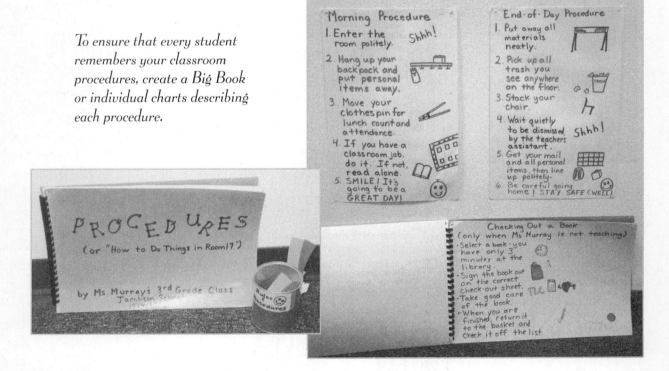

paper and have each student illustrate a page. Then I collect all the pages and bind them between two colored sheets of construction paper. I keep the Big Book handy at all times so students can refresh their memories. The procedures Big Book is a lifesaver when I get a new student—all I have to do is ask a student helper to share the information in the book with the new student. I also create slips of paper with questions about my classroom procedures on them and place them in a can. When a quick sponge activity is needed, perhaps while waiting in line for lunch, I have a student choose a procedure slip and describe or model how to complete the procedure.

Give your procedures adequate time to take hold; changing a procedure on a daily or even weekly basis doesn't give students enough time to make it a routine. If a procedure doesn't seem to be working, even though you've taught it thoroughly and children have practiced it numerous times, be flexible enough to modify or simplify it, then reteach and practice it again.

Remember to go back to *The First Days of School* by Harry and Rosemary Wong for more information on establishing procedures.

Establishing Classroom Rules

Rules are expectations for general behavior, such as "be kind," "be polite," "work hard," or "do your personal best." During the first week of school, discuss and model school and playground rules in depth, as well as the reasons for having rules and laws in every walk of life. Developing your classroom rules with student input fosters "buy-in."

After your classroom rules have been determined, teach appropriate behavior as you would an instructional objective—describe, model, give a rationale, practice, give feedback, and monitor. Have students role-play examples of following (and not following) the classroom rules, and discuss cause and effect related to the rules. Continue modeling and role playing throughout the year. You will find that even after a three-day weekend, student behavior may revert and test the strength of your resolve.

Brainstorming Rules with Primary Students

With primary students, you may want to have the whole group brainstorm what will make the classroom a good place to learn as well as a safe, happy place to be. Print student suggestions on a large piece of butcher paper so everyone can see them; draw icons if necessary. Validate all student responses by writing them on the butcher paper. You will notice that students have a tendency to state rules in the negative (e.g., "don't run") rather than the positive (e.g., "walk in the halls"). You may choose to ask them for positive ways to restate their suggestions now or after the final rules have been chosen. You may also be able to combine student responses as they are shared. When all the students' ideas have been listed, have the class consolidate them or vote on the three to five most important rules on the

Our Class Rules

Behave

Don't hit other people

Be nice ★

Do good work ★

Don't take things that aren't yours

No fighting

Don't interrupt

Help other people ★

Don't run

Don't talk back

This list of potential rules was developed by a primary class. The students voted for their three favorite rules, noted by the stars on the chart.

list to establish a reasonable number of classroom rules. Consider asking them to choose just three rules as a group and save the last for your choice—something like "do your best" or "work hard," which encompasses many behaviors. *Remember that rules are general guidelines for behavior, not specifics on how things are to be done.*

Brainstorming Rules with Intermediate Students

In an intermediate class, begin your rule-setting session by asking students why people need rules and laws. Ask them what kinds of things students should and shouldn't do to make this class the best in the whole school.

Then explain that they will be working with one another to brainstorm ideas for rules. Introduce the guidelines for brainstorming:

☼ Everyone in the group must take turns sharing ideas.

☼ The group "recorder" will do the writing; the recorder may choose to share the task with another student.

☼ Students should use their best-guess spelling when recording ideas.

☼ Students may offer only serious ideas.

☼ All serious ideas are to be written down.

☼ No put-downs are allowed.

☼ The recorder has 10 to 15 minutes to write down the group's ideas.

Divide the students into groups of three or four. Give each group a piece of 12- by 18-inch white construction paper and a marker for writing (a different color for each group). Allow students adequate time to brainstorm and record their ideas; then collect each group's lists and markers. After a break to allow for physical activity to "get the wiggles out," invite students to gather as a whole group, but sit close to the other members of their brainstorming group. Ask the first group to share their list orally with the class while you record their ideas with their marker on a large sheet of butcher paper divided into three or four columns (each

My third-grade class brainstormed these exhaustive lists of rules for our classroom. We grouped them into three main rules: Be Kind and Polite; Work Hard; Follow School Rules.

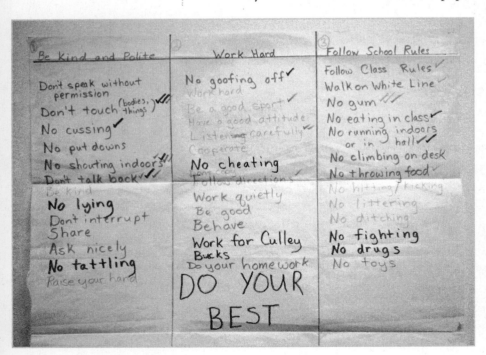

Be Kind and Polite	Work Hard	Follow School Rules
Don't speak without permission	No goofing off ✓	Follow Class Rules ✓
Don't touch (bodies, things) ✓✓	Work hard	Walk on White Line ✓
No cussing ✓	Be a good sport ✓	No gum ✓✓✓
No put downs	Have a good attitude	No eating in class ✓
No shouting indoors ✓✓	Listening carefully ✓✓	No running indoors or in hall ✓✓
Don't talk back ✓✓	Cooperate	No climbing on desk
Be Kind	No cheating	No throwing food ✓
No lying	Follow directions ✓	No hitting/kicking
Don't interrupt	Work quietly	No littering
Share	Be good	No ditching
Ask nicely	Behave	No fighting
No tattling	Work for Culley Bucks	No drugs
Raise your hand	Do your homework	No toys
	DO YOUR BEST	

column is for a generalization you have already determined but have not yet shared with the students: for example, "be kind," "work hard," and "follow school rules"). Place their ideas in the appropriate *unlabeled* column. Don't let on to students what the columns are for or what the categories are.

Every idea that is shared should relate to the general code of at least one of the columns. If an idea doesn't seem to fit anywhere, begin a separate list of miscellaneous ideas. Continue listing ideas that all the groups share, using their markers; however, if an idea is a repetition of one already shared, simply place a check mark by the original idea using the group's marker.

After all ideas are shared, you will have a rainbow-colored list reflecting the ideas of the whole class, the important ideas indicated by check marks from one or more groups. Have the whole class chorally read the first column and ask them for some words or phrases that summarize all the ideas in that column. Eventually, someone will suggest "be kind" or a similar positive statement that will become the heading for that column. Repeat with the other columns, until you have three "codes" for behavior in the classroom. Make sure that codes are stated positively; students love the word *don't*! Rewrite the three final codes—Be Kind. Work Hard. Follow School Rules.—on a piece of posterboard under the heading "Room ___'s Code of Conduct," and post it in a central location in the classroom.

Another meaningful way to develop rules with intermediate students is to create a Class Constitution. The process described above may be used to generate ideas, but you can integrate it with a unit of study about the United States Constitution so students have a good feel for how the end product should look and sound.

No matter how you decide to develop your class rules, they must be *meaningful* to you and your students. It's not enough just to say, "kind students listen" or "be respectful." To define the specifics of each class rule fully, create a Y-chart (right) and have the students brainstorm what listening (respect, sharing, and so forth) *looks like*, *sounds like*, and *feels like*. Post it on the classroom wall for the year, referring to it often and updating it as necessary. Notice students using the social skill and let them know they're using it— "I can tell that Megan is listening because her eyes are on me and her hands are still. Good remembering, Megan!"

Posting class rules helps students remember them—and abide by them. ▶

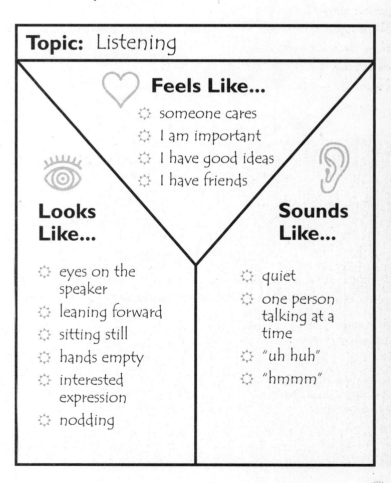

Topic: Listening

♡ **Feels Like...**
☼ someone cares
☼ I am important
☼ I have good ideas
☼ I have friends

Looks Like...
☼ eyes on the speaker
☼ leaning forward
☼ sitting still
☼ hands empty
☼ interested expression
☼ nodding

Sounds Like...
☼ quiet
☼ one person talking at a time
☼ "uh huh"
☼ "hmmm"

PART III

The First Month of School

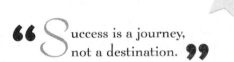

"Success is a journey, not a destination. "

—*Ben Sweetland*

TeacherVision .com has an online monthly newsletter for new teachers. You absolutely must check it out at:

www.teachervision.com /tv/lounge/newsletter /newteacher

Let's continue the journey through your first month of teaching! After the initial thrill of the first day of school, you must now continue to build your skills in classroom management, behavior management, planning, teaching, and working with parents. This section provides a peek at what lies ahead as you travel through your first weeks of teaching. As you read the information on the first month of school, keep your vision in mind. Go back and review your dream of success and your action plan. You will probably be ready to add to your action plan at this point in the year. Don't be too ambitious; remember to identify baby steps that will help you achieve your vision.

Organization: Managing the Paper Load

The more organized you are, the less frustrating the paper chase will be for you, your principal, and any substitute teachers who visit your room. I had an excellent role model for organization when I was student teaching. My master teacher made a point of never leaving school until everything was ready for the following day. She explained to me that you never know when you'll have an accident or be called out of town for an emergency. Another teacher I worked with took care of all paperwork the same day she received it; she never lost a paper or missed the due date on anything.

Because this is such a busy time of year for new teachers, it's probably not a good idea to revamp your whole system for organizing files, materials, resources, library books, and so on. Save the major reorganization for winter break and settle for a simple way to keep things orderly now without having to be perfect. A series of labeled boxes (masters to file, extra copies, things I have to do NOW, school information, things I want to order) near your desk may be just what you need to sort through all the papers that are no doubt piling up. Did you ever imagine that you would accumulate so much so fast? When your desk is overflowing and you can't spare the time to organize, consider bringing in reinforcements. A friend or family member could save you several hours (which you could spend on planning!) by helping you sort through the mountains of paperwork.

Enlisting Student Helpers

Students of all ages love to help! Prepare a student-helper system to involve your students in taking care of classroom business and the classroom itself. In kindergarten and first grade, I had a job for every child every week (many jobs, like holding those heavy classroom doors, required two students). I created a chart with graphics and job titles. The children's names were written on clothespins that I moved down the chart each week.

The system I used in third grade involved eight students per week and utilized a wall chart with library pockets for student names. To simplify the weekly changing of the jobs, I gave a laminated description of each job's responsibilities to the first student who had that job at the beginning of the year. I trained those first helpers carefully. Then the next Monday, they trained the new helpers, handing over the job description cards and assisting them during their first day on the job.

Eight jobs were plenty for my intermediate students. When I explained the classroom jobs, one of my students asked, "But what are you going to do now, Ms. Murray?" Of course, the answer was, "Teach!"

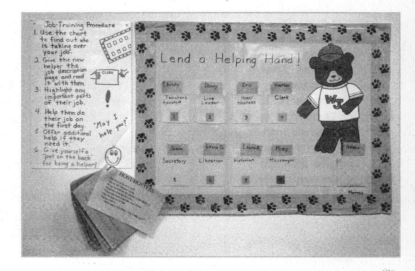

81

Each child got a chance to do every job at least once and was responsible for training someone else to do it, too. Below, I've listed the descriptions for jobs I used in my class. Think about what you want students to do.

Class Job Descriptions

- **Line Leader**—Be the first person in line; set an example for the rest of the class on how to act in the halls; stop the line at all corners; wait for the teacher's signal before you start walking.

- **Door Holder**—Hold the door for the class; close the door when the class leaves the room; help the "Caboose" carry the class lunch basket to and from lunch.

- **Host or Hostess**—Sit at the desk by the classroom door; greet visitors: "Welcome to our class. My name is _____. May I help you?"

- **Chair Manager**—When you come in first thing in the morning, quietly and carefully unstack the chairs; at the end of the day, make sure all chairs are stacked correctly.

- **Song Leader**—When you come in first thing in the morning, choose two songs you would like the class to sing; help the teacher find the tapes and CDs that go with the songs; sit in the teacher's chair and lead the singing.

- **Flag Bearer**—Ring the bell for the Pledge of Allegiance; when all students are standing respectfully, get the flag and hold it at attention; say, "Ready, begin," and lead the class in the Pledge; put the flag away carefully.

- **Teacher's Assistant**—Help the teacher with daily reviews (e.g., math calendar, Mountain Math); do special jobs for the teacher; help the teacher reward student work and behavior with stickers or stamps.

- **Chooser**—Choose students who are sitting politely to go to their desks, come to the front of the room, line up, or go to centers.

- **Secretary**—Check the attendance and lunch board (see page 52); mark the lunch-count slip and give it to the "Messenger"; pass out papers and other materials.

- **Mail Person**—Deliver class mail and papers to go home; make sure that all mail is picked up before the students leave the classroom at the end of the day.

- **Messenger**—Take the lunch count to the lunchroom; take the attendance folder to the office; deliver and pick up any messages.

- **Room Checker**—Check to make sure the room is in good condition after each activity; remind students who leave materials or trash out to put them in their proper place; at the end of the day, make sure that all materials are put away neatly and all trash is in the trash can.

- **Librarian**—Put returned books back on the shelves in the correct place; make sure that the class library is clean and that the books are neatly organized and in good shape; give torn books to the teacher to be fixed.

- **Historian**—Write down what we do in class every day; tell students who were absent what they missed; draw what we did last week on a time-line page (you may do this during writing time and your free time).

- **Pencil Sharpener**—At the beginning of each day, sharpen the pencils that were put in the "need sharpening" can; empty the pencil sharpener into the trash can.

- **Caboose**—Be the last person in line; set an example for the rest of the class on how to act in the halls; help the "Door Holder" carry the class lunch basket to and from lunch.

- **Substitute**—Do the jobs for any student helpers who are absent.

Some intermediate teachers have their students apply and even go through interviews to get classroom jobs. This integrates well with social studies units on economics and careers. Other intermediate teachers select one child each day or each week to be their "teacher's assistant" who is responsible for all jobs that need to be done during that time period.

Providing Encouragement

Today's children live in an increasingly negative world. Instead of humor, we use sarcasm. Instead of kind words, children hear put-downs. Instead of warm and respectful physical contact, children are sometimes shoved and hit.

Encouragement helps students believe in themselves and their abilities. It enables them to accept and learn from their mistakes while developing a risk-taking attitude. Encouragement is essential to learning, even to survival.

Set Realistic Expectations

Let's take a moment to think about those things that can wither a child's self-esteem. The first is negative expectations. We communicate our expectations physically and verbally. If I walk into the room lethargically, look around disinterestedly, and slump down in my chair, I am conveying the expectation that little of interest is going to occur here. If I tell someone, "Just do the best you can on this project and I'll fix it up for you," I am telling him that he is incapable. Strive to eliminate the negative from your vocabulary, facial expressions, and physical demeanor.

On the other side of the coin, unreasonably high standards have a negative impact. If we expect children to exceed their abilities with no extra support from us, we set them up to fail. Instead, consciously hold all students in high esteem and demonstrate your belief in them. Design

> *A child needs encouragement as a plant needs water.*
>
> —*Rudolf Dreikurs*

Dreikurs and Dinkmeyer have written several books dealing with classroom behavior and encouragement. Any title by these authors will be worth reading.

learning situations that build on their strengths and foster success. The caring and respect you show will serve as a model for peer relationships as well. You can provide the support students need by:

- emphasizing cooperation and collaborative learning

- pairing students based on their strengths and challenges in content areas, learning styles, and multiple intelligences

- promoting cross-age tutoring, so everyone can succeed

At the same time, we need to let students know that it's okay to take risks. Publicly admit mistakes you make as a teacher, correct them, and use them as an opportunity for learning. I mark correct (rather than incorrect) answers, calculating grades as a fraction with the number *right* over the number *attempted* (+9/10). After all, how helpful is it to a student who slaves over a math paper, finishes only 10 of the problems but gets 9 of the 10 correct, to then receive an "F" because there were 40 problems on the page?

Appreciate Each Student

Let's examine ways that teachers can encourage children in the classroom. Start by appreciating differences and unique qualities in each student and treating everyone equally. Separate the behavior from the child to teach him or her guidelines while maintaining a quality relationship. This means that if a child behaves appropriately, he or she is not labeled as "good" in general, and if he or she behaves inappropriately, he or she is not labeled "bad" in general. Find something to encourage in each child, every day, by focusing on progress and effort. And when you make accepting remarks to students, don't qualify them with a "but," "however," or "if you only...."

Make reasonable accommodations for your students. In *The Little Prince* by Antoine de Saint Exupery, an eccentric king says, "One must require from each one the duty which each one can perform." To make this work:

- know your students' needs and capabilities

- help them celebrate each success, no matter how small

- reduce competition by helping each student set personal goals for academics and behavior

- allow students to self-evaluate their performance on a regular basis rather than always having them rely on your judgment

- hold conferences with your students during the school year to assist them in talking about their strengths and goals

- model effective evaluation skills for the whole class by sharing your writing with them and asking them for comments; ask for positive comments first and then for questions regarding your work

Things We Do and Say
to Encourage Children

THINGS WE DO...	THINGS WE SAY...
☼ give a pat on the back	☼ How do you feel?
☼ share YOUR feelings	☼ What do you think?
☼ listen, really listen, to the child's stories	☼ What can I do to help?
☼ give each child time to himself or herself	☼ I really enjoyed your company.
☼ have a special day for each child	☼ Let's talk about it.
☼ accept the child as he or she is	☼ Tell me about it.
☼ give the child an opportunity to try	☼ You really helped me.
☼ talk *to* the child, not *at* her or him	☼ Let's try it together.
☼ let the child make decisions and accept them	☼ You can do it!
☼ forget past problems	☼ I'm glad you're here.
☼ always use a kind tone of voice	☼ Try it.
☼ use warm facial and body expressions	☼ Well done!
☼ shake a hand	☼ I need your help.
☼ smile, wink, or nod	☼ I'm impressed with _____.
☼ acknowledge feelings	☼ You are very special.
☼ look at the child	☼ What did you like best about today?
☼ be interested	☼ I like your smile.
☼ be there when a child needs you	☼ You always make me laugh!
☼ show the child that you trust her or him	☼ I believe you can do it.
☼ challenge the child	☼ Believe in yourself.
☼ ask for the child's opinion	☼ You're such a good worker.
☼ share responsibilities	☼ You do _____ so well.
☼ tell the child and show that she or he belongs	☼ Don't give up.
☼ refrain from criticism	☼ You're so nice to be around.
☼ celebrate small efforts	☼ Do the very best you can do.
☼ appreciate uniqueness	☼ How can we fix it?
☼ review accomplishments	☼ What did you add to the group?
☼ build on strengths	☼ Thank you for being kind.
☼ share ideas	☼ I liked working with you today.
☼ make an appointment to spend time with each child	☼ You are special because _____.

Additional help in behavior management is right next door at your school. Ask for help! Talk to other teachers about how they handle similar situations. Find out if your school has some kind of formal assistance program for teachers experiencing behavior challenges. Sitting down with a group of professionals who are willing to share ideas with you is certainly worthwhile. Let your peers be involved in helping you find solutions; never say, "I've tried everything!"

Reinforcing Rules and Procedures

To reinforce your rules and procedures, you must be consistent, firm, and fair in their application. Some days you will need to make a conscious effort to be consistent, as it is sometimes easier to let little things go than to deal with them. If you overlook misapplication of rules and procedures, the glue that holds your classroom together will begin to weaken. Encourage your students and refer to the rules when students apply them to their daily experiences in the classroom: "Who can tell me which rule Brian demonstrated when he held the door for the rest of the class?"

Capitalize on the power of peers by having students look for others who follow the rules and giving them opportunities to share their positive observations with the rest of the class. If you hold class meetings, there could be a time to share "Compliments." You could provide students with paper-chain strips on which they write compliments related to rules and procedures or even just the names of the students who earned the compliment. Have students read the strips and connect them to the class "Compliment Chain." If your class is indeed focused on the positive, the chain will cross the room multiple times during the year.

Involve parents in the reinforcement of your rules and procedures by letting them know what you expect of their children. During the first week of school, you will want to send home your discipline plan. As the year continues, inform the parents of the things their children are doing well, in addition to areas that need more work. You can send a special note home or call parents in the evening to share something positive their child did at school. Parents are always shocked (and pleased!) when the teacher calls home to say something good about their child.

Using Rewards

There is a continual debate in education over the value of extrinsic reinforcement. Alfie Kohn suggests that we are "punished by rewards" in his book of that title, and argues that we need to move "beyond bribes, threats, and competition." Others believe in reinforcement wholeheartedly. In my experience, sometimes reinforcement is appropriate and sometimes it's not. If you have defined and established your classroom procedures and deliver high-quality lessons, many of your behavior challenges will be proactively eliminated. But what about those students who just don't respond to the things you've tried? What about the students who reject your attempts at encouragement? What about the students who behave worse after you point out their positive attributes? When you have exhausted all other options, rewards or consequences may help you get the student in question back on track.

The use of rewards should be limited and should always be tied to an intrinsic motivator, such as the pleasure of a job well done. There are several types of positive reinforcers:

- ⚙ **Symbols**—letter grades, stars, stickers, stamps
- ⚙ **Recognition**—displays of student work, awards, certificates, verbal recognition
- ⚙ **Activities**—free reading time, game time, lunch with teacher, teacher's helper, the chance to be first in line, fast-food coupons

My favorite rewards are those that require little or no money and provide for extended teacher-student interactions. For example, "lunch with teacher" was a highly coveted pass to receive in my classroom (see page 90). I didn't buy their lunch or give them a special snack; we just ate together and chatted. You will find that extra time together outside of the classroom routine can enrich the relationship between you and your students. It can also give you greater insight into their personalities and problems. How wonderful that something free can be so meaningful!

Words of Fortune

I usually started off the year with a whole-group incentive to build a feeling of class collaboration. Words of Fortune was my favorite. I chose a surprise event for the entire class to earn. I drew spaces for each letter in the name of the event. At first, I did this on the chalkboard; then, I made a Words of Fortune board so my spaces wouldn't accidentally be erased. Each time the class received a compliment as a whole, or completed a task well (behaviorally or academically), I filled in one letter. Since students love to solve puzzles, I provided a "guessing can" where students could deposit their written guesses just for the fun of it. I asked them not to tell anyone what they thought so the surprise wouldn't be spoiled for the rest of the class. When the entire puzzle was completed, the whole class earned the prize, which usually involved an event such as "dress-up day" or "popcorn party." You can make the puzzle longer by adding "on Friday" or some other qualifier.

Our school mascot helped promote effective collaboration.

Team Incentives

Occasionally during the year, I used Team Incentives to promote working together. I tried to be specific about the positive behaviors I noticed when giving stamps, stickers, or marks to teams that exhibited good teamwork: "Thank you, Team 1, for showing caring" or "Team 4, thank you for stacking your chairs quickly and quietly." At the end of the week, the team that had earned the most points won. The prize was usually lunch with teacher, although sometimes I sweetened the deal by adding another special privilege such as "write on the chalkboard" while they were having lunch with me. I tried to shift my teams on a regular basis so that their composition varied. If you find students getting angry at one or two teammates who misbehave, competition is getting too strong.

Behavior Bucks

At other times I used individual incentives rather than whole-group or team incentives. Behavior Bucks (see page 182) are a form of class money that individuals earn for doing their job as students (displaying appropriate behavior, turning in homework, and so on). I enjoyed holding periodic auctions so the children could spend their Bucks. Students brought in discarded items for the auction, and I donated notebooks, pencils, paint sets, fast-food gift certificates, as well as several passes; one year a "Help the Teacher Teach a Lesson" pass sold for 125 Bucks! At the end of the year, I put books that the class has co-created on the auction block. After each auction was concluded, I gave students 10 to 15 minutes to trade the items they had bought with other students; they enjoyed this almost as much as the actual auction. If you choose to have an auction, be sure to have plenty of items to auction off as well as a large block of time so every student has an opportunity to join the fun.

Behavior Bucks for K

With kindergartners, I had each student color and cut out five Behavior Bucks to place on a chart; these were their five "chances" for the week, and they could earn additional Bucks by bringing back homework, helping other students, and so forth. If a student chose not to follow the rule we were focusing on during the week, he or she paid me one Buck. At the end of the week, anyone who had at least one Buck left got to select a prize—rarely did anyone lose all their Bucks in a week. I invited students with the most Bucks at the end of the week to visit the prize table first, which was an incentive in itself. At the beginning of the year with kindergartners, the reward needed to be distributed on a daily rather than weekly basis to give them immediate feedback on their behavior.

Chance Jar

Another individual incentive that can be effective is the "I've Been Caught Being Good" chance slip (see page 182). Distribute chance slips to students with a word of encouragement to reinforce their positive behavior. When students receive chance slips, they write their names on the back of the slips and place them in the class Chance Jar. I held drawings at the end of each week, again offering more coupons and passes than tangible rewards. I set out all the prizes —maybe five to ten a week (remember, most of them don't cost me a penny)—and the first person whose name was drawn got to choose a prize first, and so on. A student helper drew the names, called them out, and tore up the slips when the winners came forward to claim their prizes. If a student whose name was called didn't want any of the prizes offered that week, I placed their winning-chance slip back into the jar for next week's drawing. I emptied the jar once a month. Be generous when distributing chance slips so every student has an opportunity to be lucky!

Keeping Positive

To keep your rewards from being punishments, deliver them fairly and in a positive manner to those earning the rewards—and *not* as a punishment to those not earning them. A "so there" attitude when reinforcing behavior destroys class morale and student self-esteem. Rewards will be ineffective if they are too easily earned, too difficult to attain, or meaningless to the student. You may find it necessary to change your system of reinforcement throughout the year to maintain its effectiveness.

Staying on Target

Reward systems can overwhelm the teacher. When I first started teaching, I spent so much time passing out slips, marking team points, and rewarding the whole class all at once that I barely had time to teach! Keep in mind that the goal of using rewards is to promote positive behavior so students can learn. *If your students don't need them, then don't use them.* Refuse to use too many reward systems at once; you won't have time to teach. I finally discovered that a simple whole-class system like Words of Fortune, supplemented by an additional reinforcement program for the handful of students who needed more feedback, was sufficient for most of the school year.

One final caution: When you hear students asking, "What do I get if…" you'll know they've been over-rewarded. Take a step back and think about how you can get your students to take responsibility for their own behavior instead of having to constantly reward them into behaving appropriately. As a society, we cannot afford to create citizens who will only do what's expected if there is a material reward for doing it.

Remember that the investment of your time and attention is one of the most desired rewards. Simple and sincere encouragement goes a long way toward keeping student behavior positive.

Before you go out and buy things to use as rewards, check out the list on page 90. Students will enjoy some of these rewards even more than things you can buy!

Consequences

Rewards are only one part of an effective management system. With some children, positive reinforcement just doesn't work. In that case, you may try to extinguish the behavior by ignoring it, then use a positive reinforcer at times when the student chooses to behave appropriately. Let's say, for example, that Billy is highly impulsive. When he wants to talk, he talks. The principle of extinction requires you to ignore his impulsive talking until he remembers to raise his hand; then you thank him immediately for controlling himself and let him share. Ignoring behaviors can be difficult at times. My suggestion is to use extinction for *one* behavior at a time; if you also ignored Billy's impulsive touching, running, and pushing, he wouldn't get any of your attention at all. If neither system seems to be working, a negative reinforcer, such as natural or logical consequences, may be used.

Consequences help children define inappropriate behavior and what effect

Rich Rewards on a Poor Pocketbook

- ☼ a smile
- ☼ a pat or handshake
- ☼ a positive phone call home
- ☼ lunch with teacher
- ☼ help the teacher teach a lesson
- ☼ sit in the teacher's desk for one day
- ☼ game time
- ☼ take care of classroom pets
- ☼ use clay during free time
- ☼ choose any class job for the day
- ☼ decorate a bulletin board
- ☼ read to a younger child
- ☼ no homework for the day
- ☼ be first to go to lunch or recess
- ☼ coupon from McDonald's or Taco Bell
- ☼ a three-minute, uninterrupted talk with the teacher
- ☼ stay in at recess to play a game with a friend

- ☼ a high five
- ☼ a positive note home
- ☼ lunch with your favorite person
- ☼ sit in a different seat for one day
- ☼ be teacher's assistant for the day
- ☼ free time to draw
- ☼ theme day—dress up in costume
- ☼ draw on the chalkboard
- ☼ be the first in line
- ☼ be a helper in another classroom
- ☼ help the custodian
- ☼ use stamps and ink pads
- ☼ use the tape recorder to tape a story
- ☼ earn a certificate
- ☼ earn a badge
- ☼ keep the class mascot/trophy on your desk for the day
- ☼ bring in a tape or CD of your choice to play during free time

Teaching with Love and Logic by Jim Fay explores the use of logical consequences in the classroom. Fay also writes books for parents that are good additions to any library.

that behavior has. Natural consequences are the result of a violation of the *natural order* of events. For example, if I don't set my alarm clock, I am late for school; if I don't wear my coat, I am cold. Logical consequences are the result of a violation of the *social order*. For example, if I don't do my homework, I get a "0"; if I throw trash on the playground, I spend recess picking up trash. Both types of consequences can be highly effective at helping children recognize limits at school.

The following guidelines are helpful in creating and implementing effective consequences:

- ☼ The student must truly understand your expectations for classroom work and behavior. Ensure that students know your expectations by modeling and practicing them frequently.

- ☼ The student must have the skills to meet your expectations. Should a child with ADHD have to sit still at a desk for an hour?

- The student must understand the reasons he or she is expected to behave in certain ways. "Because I said so…" just doesn't work in the classroom. Explain and demonstrate the reasoning behind your requests.

- The student must understand ahead of time the probable consequences of specific behaviors. "Fighting is a serious misbehavior; if you are fighting for any reason, you will immediately go to the Problem-Solving Station."

- The student must view the consequence as a negative. Staying in the classroom with the teacher at recess for detention may be a *positive* thing to some students.

- The student must have the opportunity to choose to behave appropriately. "Would you like to continue working with the group or go back to your seat during the project? Your behavior will let me know which you choose."

- The teacher-student interaction at the time the consequence is delivered must not in itself be punishing, but should be calm and logical. "I've had enough! Go to the office immediately!" is its own reward; the child has caused the teacher to lose it. Instead, try "Sarah, your behavior is showing me that you have made the choice to…"

- Consequences that are too harsh or too frequently used place the teacher in direct opposition to the student and invite criticism from parents. All negatives should be balanced with a positive to improve both student behavior and self-esteem.

Consequences can take several forms. The consequence of *losing a privilege* can be made to fit the transgression. For example, if a child plays during work time, then he should work during play time. *Fines* can be charged as a consequence by having the student give up Behavior Bucks or other incentives. Use caution with this—many believe that once an incentive is earned, it should not be taken away. *Restitution*, or paying for damage or repair, is another type of consequence. If a student loses a library book, she will have to pay for it. *Confiscation* is a favorite consequence of teachers. Each of these types of consequences can be devastating for children, so be sure to give them the opportunity to choose their behavior before imposing a consequence. If I ask a student to put away a toy and show me that he chooses to be a learner, and he doesn't, *then* I will enforce a consequence. Teaching students about making choices empowers them and teaches them how to make good decisions.

When implementing consequences, don't make them seem like punishments. Students don't develop lifelong learning skills via punishment, but through the opportunity to choose behavior and accept the positive or negative consequences. Children tend to view punishment as a statement of your dislike for them. Punishment rarely works beyond the moment or outside the classroom when the teacher is not present. It is sometimes used as an immediate intervention, but doesn't typically create change. In contrast, natural and logical consequences are completely related to the

t is no doubt time for you to take a break! In the movie *A Christmas Story*, Ralphie's teacher has a drawerful of toys and objects inappropriate for the classroom. Even if it's not close to Christmas yet, head to your nearest movie rental store and treat yourself to a little classroom management, 1950s-style.

behavior. For example, the student who chooses to misbehave during group activities needs to adjust his behavior before rejoining the group; the student who studies for a test has a better chance of doing well. Just a note of caution: *Don't expect all of your behavior challenges to be fixed the first time you implement logical choice.* Be patient with your students and yourself and celebrate the baby steps along the way. To use logical consequences:

1. Establish guidelines in the classroom. Your classroom rules define behavioral and academic limits and expectations for students.

2. When a student violates the class guidelines, offer him or her a logical choice: "Would you prefer to continue playing the game, or do you need to sit out for a few minutes? What is your choice?" In the case of some misbehaviors, the student owns the problem, and teacher intervention is not required. For example, if a student forgets her lunch, it is not necessary for the teacher to implement a consequence; the natural order of events will provide the consequence. If a student is engaging in minor misbehavior that is not keeping those around him or her from working, the teacher may choose not to implement a consequence.

3. Watch the student's behavior to see what choice has been made before implementing a consequence. This gives the student an opportunity to be responsible and correct his own behavior.

4. If the behavior stops, follow through with encouragement: "I'm glad that you have chosen to continue playing the game with us." If the behavior persists, follow through with the consequence: "I can see by your behavior that you have chosen to take a break from our game. We'll try again in a few minutes. Let me know when you're ready to try again." Do not allow your tone to be punishing or hostile. A simple, matter-of-fact statement will show the student that you respect him *and* yourself.

5. Offer the student a chance to wipe out the past. As in the previous example, after two to five minutes, ask the student if he is ready to rejoin the game. Your demeanor must not be irritated, angry, hurt, or frustrated. Now, focus on the student's *positive* behavior.

Weekly Point Card

The Weekly Point Card (see page 183) is a method of monitoring both positive and negative consequences. This student-managed behavior tool is appropriate for second through fourth graders. Choose five positive characteristics to write in the five spaces for description, such as "uses self-control," "is responsible," "follows school rules," "cooperates," "completes class work," "listens attentively," "helps others," "works hard," "is organized," and "completes homework." Every Monday, students receive a copy of the point card to be placed on their desks. Used as

It's my turn now! Classroom management issues can get you down during the first few months of school. Remember the New Teacher Cycle on page 14? It's definitely time for you to get away so you can clear your mind, if only for a day. Grab a friend or family member and take a day trip, even if it's to your local spa, museum, or park. Your work will still be there when you get back, but you'll have greater internal resources to deal with the day-to-day stresses if you take time out for yourself!

positive reinforcement, points are tallied each day as the individual student displays the qualities valued in your classroom. At the end of the week, tallies are totaled, and the teacher or student writes a comment summarizing the student's behavior and work. Follow up by sending the Friday Report home for parent signature and comments, to be returned the following Monday.

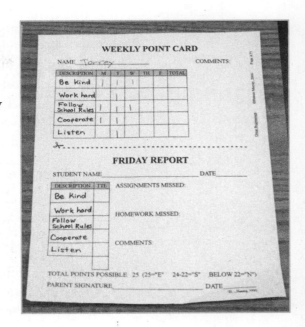

Baseball Behavior Card

A system for recording inappropriate behavior is the Baseball Behavior Card (see page 184). For your *one or two students* who don't seem to recognize what is appropriate or inappropriate behavior, select one behavior you want them to improve over a period of a week or two. Have the student cross off a baseball each time he demonstrates the inappropriate behavior. You must focus on just one behavior. If the baseball sheet becomes a catchall for everything the student does wrong, he will always be "out." Be sure to involve the student in setting the consequence for crossing off each baseball.

The Weekly Point Card helps students monitor their behavior and work.

Problem-Solving Notebook

I kept a Problem-Solving Notebook on a time-out table and dated a new page each day. As a problem occurred, I directed the misbehaving child to take a few minutes to write about the problem in the notebook. This allowed me to complete lessons with minimum disturbance and served as excellent documentation of student misbehavior. The Problem-Solving Notebook helps the student see the teacher as a partner in problem solving, not as someone waiting for the student to make a mistake. The key to effective use of this tool is the method of delivery by the teacher. "Johnny, get over there to the Problem-Solving Notebook right now and write down why you are being so rude today!" is not appropriate; instead say, "Johnny, I need to help the rest of the class get started on this project. Would you please take a few minutes to write in the Problem-Solving Notebook about what just happened? I'll be there in a few minutes to help you work through it." It is important to follow up on what your students write as soon as you can get the rest of the class working *and* get yourself calmed down.

No matter what subject or grade you teach, making learning interesting and active will maximize the effectiveness of your teaching and minimize the disruptions of student misbehavior. Students will enjoy learning so much, they will forget to act inappropriately!

The Problem-Solving Notebook is a great management tool, and it helps kids think about their behavior.

We know that thorough planning and preparation are directly correlated to success in teaching. Teaming up to plan with another teacher (or two) who has a philosophy similar to yours can save you a great deal of time and help you generate wonderful lessons. Such a partnership can be helpful if the partners have different strengths instructionally and organizationally. My last planning partners were the perfect team members for me. One was great at dealing with our field trip and special-event paperwork and phone calls, and the other came up with exciting, hands-on activities for our cross-age tutoring, while I enjoyed producing student plays for our cooperative theme. The three of us worked together during one planning period each week to brainstorm the activities we would like to do. This powerful collaboration gave each of us added energy to teach actively and meaningfully.

If co-planning is not for you, place a "help wanted" note in the lounge at your school stating topics and resources you need. Don't be surprised if you find lots of good materials and some new planning partners. Most teachers I know are more than willing to share resources and ideas. You can meet after school, on weekends, on the phone, or via the Internet. You don't have to work at the same site to plan together!

Long-Range Plans: Five Steps to Keep You on Track All Year

One aspect of planning in many school districts is developing long-range plans that serve as an instructional map to guide you through the year. Creating long-range plans is a lengthy and complex process—don't expect to finish them in a day! Ask the teachers in your grade level if they do long-range planning together. If not, plan with one other teacher at your grade level. If that isn't feasible, choose a teacher from another grade level with whom you work well and plan your science, social studies, and health instruction together. You'll still need to determine the literacy and mathematics plans for your own grade level, but at least you'll have support during the rest of the planning process.

Even if your school doesn't require long-range plans, I still recommend that you go through your grade-level curriculum and list the skills and concepts that you plan to teach each month of the year. This process will familiarize you with what you are required to teach and give you the whole picture so the rhythm of the year isn't a mystery to you. If the concept of having a year-long plan seems too structured for you, remember that it is simply a plan from which you may deviate. Equate your long-range plan to mapping out a cross-country road trip; you are free to take side trips, but it sure helps to know where you're ultimately headed!

Step 1: Choose a Format and Collect Your Materials To create long-range plans, begin by asking your principal how he or she would like to see your long-range plans formatted and whether there is an example you could see. There are sections of two sample formats on page 97. When you sit down to determine your overall plan for the year, have a copy of your state and district standards, objectives, and benchmarks close by so you can determine an appropriate sequence for teaching all identified skills and concepts. You will also need to have teacher's guides and other grade-level materials on hand for easy reference.

Step 2: Mark Your Calendar Start with a blank calendar. Make note of your school schedule, including holidays, celebrations, track breaks (if year-round), grading period dates, testing times, and schoolwide activities. Mark off a few extra days around these times, as they will most likely impact your instructional day. Also, set aside time for periodic skill review, assessment, and for practicing test-taking skills. At this point, you'll have a clear picture of the actual time you have available for instruction. Isn't it amazing how short a school year actually is?

Step 3: Focus on Content Begin sifting through your science, social studies, and health curriculums to determine what time of year would be best to study specific content. Write the objectives in the appropriate spaces on your calendar. For example, don't schedule your unit on plants in January—March, April, or May are better times for observing plant changes in many climates. Planning to study light and shadows in February may work well since your lessons can be related to Groundhog Day. Many teachers study cultures in November and December—it's a good time to look at traditions of people around the world.

Look through the materials that your school and grade level have available for studying the content areas. Check their readability to determine whether your students will be successful with the materials at the time you have planned to use them. Adjust topics on your calendar as necessary. For example, if you teach third grade and need to do a unit on plants, you could choose any of the spring months for optimal growing. If you have access to *The Plant That Ate Dirty Socks* as a literature set, you might opt for placing your plant unit in May, as the book can be difficult reading for some third graders.

Step 4: Integrate Language Arts and Math Once your content has been determined for the year, you can begin plugging in literacy and mathematics objectives. Continue perusing the student materials available (literature sets, Big Books, textbooks, supplementary materials) and search for basic skills that might be pulled out of the materials for teaching them in context. For example, let's say you have decided to teach a life science unit to your third graders at the beginning of the year. You have planned to have them observe the life cycle of frogs as a part of the unit. Your school has a class set of *Frog and Toad Are Friends* available, and it is easy enough to use when your students start school in the fall. You read

Several years ago, I found a book called *Do You Know What Day Tomorrow Is?* by Hopkins and Arenstein. It contains a thorough compilation of historical events and holidays for each day of the year, which helped me organize my long-range plans.

through the book and find that there are few contractions in it. Since contractions are in your third-grade curriculum, you decide to teach that skill at the beginning of the year by having your students locate non-contractions in the book (*cannot, I will, you would*) and change them to contractions that make it flow better (*can't, I'll, you'd*). You might also focus on sorting in math at that time (using buttons), since one of the Frog and Toad stories is about a lost button that the characters try to find or replace. This is also a good opener for a discussion on attributes and observations. Be aware that not all literacy and mathematics objectives are easily integrated with themes. Set aside time for your students to learn and practice those objectives that defy integration.

☼ **Step 5: Step Back and Evaluate** Now take a look at your completed calendar. It is probably a mess! So many objectives…so little time! Before you transfer your plans to the final planning pages, you may need to do some adjusting. For example, if December looks a little full, move some of the objectives to other times of the year. Remember that you and your students will be very busy around the winter holidays. Trying to cram too much instruction into a short amount of time will result in shallow learning of skills and concepts.

Once you have made all necessary adjustments, transfer the information on the calendar to your planning pages. Creating a table like the plans on page 97 with any word-processing program will facilitate this step.

Y ou may be thinking, "Why don't I just skip the calendar step and write the plans on the planning pages from the start?" Trust me…it is incredibly helpful to see it on a calendar first. Your plans will be much better organized and will flow more comfortably if you see the whole picture of your year while doing your initial long-range planning.

Long-Range Planning Checklist

— Find out what long-range plans should look like for your district or state.

— Have a copy of the standards/objectives/benchmarks for your grade level available.

— Have teacher's guides and grade-level instructional materials on hand.

— Have a pencil (and an eraser!), a blank calendar, and pages on which to write your final plans.

— Mark important dates that will impact your instruction on the calendar.

— Plan for science, social studies, and health:

— decide what time of year is best for studying each content-area objective

— check the readability of grade-level student materials for content-area instruction

— Plan for literacy and mathematics:

— use state or district benchmarks (or information on cognitive development from Piaget and other theorists) to determine an appropriate time line for teaching literacy and math skills

— check the readability of grade-level student materials for literacy

— check prerequisites for understanding mathematical concepts

— review and adjust your calendar to prevent instructional overload at busy times of the year

— Create your final plan.

— Look at your long-range plans every week as you prepare lesson plans.

Sample Long-Range Plans—Matrix Format for Science

Code	Essential Skills, Concepts, Experiences	Aug	Sep	Oct	Nov	Dec	Jan	Feb	Mar	Apr	May	Jun	Jul
1.1	compare, test, measure, record, and describe observable properties of rocks and minerals		/										
1.2	compare, measure, record, and describe air temperature, wind direction/speed, and precipitation to identify patterns over time												
1.3	observe and describe the sun, moon, and stars												
2.1	observe and describe plants and animals in their habitats												
2.2	describe the ways plants and animals adapt to their changing environments												
2.3	compare needs of living things and how those needs are met												
2.4	identify ways to conserve natural resources												
3.1	investigate changes of state of matter (solid, liquids, gases)												

Check with your administrator to find out if long-range plans are required. Even if they're optional, spend time on this worthy activity.

Sample Long-Range Plans—Traditional Format for Three Months

LANGUAGE

SEPTEMBER

1.1 good listener
1.2, 5.42 follow multiple oral directions
1.7, 5.10 listen for many purposes
1.8, 5.3 activate prior knowledge
1.9, 5.2 listen to different music and literature
2.5 interact verbally
2.8 make introductions
3.1 prewriting strategies
3.2 generate many ideas for topic
3.6 produce first draft
5.1 read silently daily
5.38 select books of choice

OCTOBER

1.3 compare and contrast sounds, rhythms, and words
1.6, 5.7, 3.4 purpose for reading, listening, and writing
2.4 many forms of oral communication
2.6. give/restate 3-step directions
3.3 generate possible writing topics
3.9 revise a written draft
4.1 legible manuscript
5.5, 5.30 describe and classify information
5.6 compare objects, pictures and words
5.7, 28 predict and provide rationale
5.24 identify story elements
5.31 real versus make-believe

NOVEMBER

1.4, 5.21,22 recall sequence
2.2 use complete sentences
3.7, 4.11 write for many purposes
3.8 respond to another's writing
3.10 rewrite a written composition
3.11 edit a composition
3.12 rewrite a composition
4.7 summarize information
5.23 identify and restate details
5.13 use familiar words to make meaning
5.26 identify author's purpose

MATH

SEPTEMBER

1.1, 3.2 sort and classify objects, shapes, and numbers
1.3 recognize and develop patterns
1.11 communicate mathematically
3.1 relative positions
4.2, 3, 4 linear measurement
5.1,2,3,4 quantity
5.14, 15, 16, 17 addition and subtraction strategies and recall

OCTOBER

1.2 use mathematical statements
3.3 geometric properties
3.4 relate geometry to environment
4.2,3,4,6,7 time
5.5,6 number composition
5.8 multidigit addition and subtraction

NOVEMBER

2.1 collect/organize/record data
2.2 construct graphs/tables/charts
2.3 interpret graphs/tables/charts
4.2,3,4 weight and mass
4.11 area and perimeter
5.7,9 number relationships and sequence
5.10 estimate quantities using objects

SOCIAL STUDIES

SEPTEMBER

1.13 why communities require laws
6.33 respect others' property and space
6.34 distinguish between facts and assumptions about others' behavior

OCTOBER

6.35 compromise in problem resolution
6.36 role of negotiation in settling disputes
3.19 read map legends
3.20 hemisphere/continent/ocean on maps/globes

NOVEMBER

5.11 life in early American communities
5.12 patriotism in American history

As you get ready to create your lesson plans each week, review your long-range plans. They will help you stay on target throughout the year so you don't get stuck on any one topic. Remember that your long-range plan is not set in stone—adjust it for "teachable moments" and remediation if necessary. Next year's planning will be much easier if you make notes about how the timing worked during your first year of teaching.

Schedule for Instruction

Now that you have an overall plan for the school year, you will need to create a general schedule of the subjects and special classes your students will participate in on a weekly basis. Your weekly schedule may fluctuate somewhat during the year, but you should have a fairly stable plan for the time spent on each subject by the end of the first two weeks of school. A weekly schedule provides you with a time structure for planning lessons. It also helps create a comfortable routine for the students so they can focus on learning.

A traditional schedule divides your day by subject areas—literacy, math, science, social studies, health, computers. An integrated format allows larger chunks of time for combinations of subjects—literacy, thematic instruction, math or science. Talk to your principal about the weekly schedule format that he or she prefers and ask for examples that can guide you in creating your own. As with long-range plans, you may wish to create your weekly schedule in a word-processing program with a table.

You will also need to find out if your district or state has mandated the amount of time required to teach each subject on a daily or weekly basis. For example, in my district, teachers are expected to spend a minimum of 140 minutes per day on literacy and 70 minutes per day on mathematics. The other subjects are more flexible and may be integrated. If there is no such standard for your state or district, you will definitely need to talk to other teachers at your grade level about the time they typically spend on each subject area.

Place times for lunch and recess, all known special classes (art, music, P.E., library, computer lab) and pullout programs (ESL, GATE, special education, speech) on a copy of your weekly schedule form—either your school's standard form or one you've created yourself. Be aware that some of these classes may not yet be scheduled and will have to be coordinated with your existing weekly schedule after the school year begins.

Think about how you would like to begin the day. Enriching, mentally stimulating activities (silent or paired reading, teacher Read Aloud, writing or journaling, singing, poetry) get students off to a good start. With primary students, we sang, recited poetry, and had students "buddy buzz" about something interesting that had happened to them on the way to school. In the intermediate grades, I began the day with 10 to 15 minutes of silent reading, after which the students wrote a one-paragraph summary as an assessment. This gave me precious time to deal with notes from parents, collect homework, and even work with students one-on-one while ensuring that the class was meaningfully engaged.

Think about what type of activity would be appropriate right after lunch. I preferred to have students write at that time. Even if a child didn't have a story to write, he or she could certainly script out what happened at lunch and recess. It was a good way to get students to be calm and cool. I scheduled some days for writing alone and others for writing with a partner. Then I used this independent work time to conference with individual students about their writing.

Think about how you would like to end the day. Too often, we are rushed as the day ends, and children leave feeling hassled and confused. I gave my students an opportunity to reflect upon what we did and learned during the day, so they went home with something to talk about with their parents. Some ways of doing this include:

'm in Charge of Celebrations by Byrd Baylor is a lovely book that introduces students to the concept of a Celebration Journal.

☼ Brainstorm what happened during the day with the whole group.

☼ Have students tell one thing they learned or did as they get in line.

☼ Have students write an individual "celebration" about something that happened to them during the school day. Teachers of young students may choose to do Celebration Journals as a whole-group shared writing activity at the end of each day (similar to "Daily News").

After considering the overall flow of the day, begin placing subjects at appropriate places in the schedule. This is a process of trial and error and can be frustrating. Place subjects carefully, looking at the interactive nature of each, which students will be out of the classroom at that time, and when your students tend to need a shift in activity structures. A few examples are:

☼ After my students read independently at their desks, I provided them with a change to whole-group instruction by having them come to the carpeted area of the room and sit on the floor for math calendar. Then, I scheduled small-group time using flexible-skill grouping to provide a balance of structures.

Schedule for Instruction Checklist

— Find out what a schedule for instruction should look like for your state or district.

— Have a copy of any recommendations or requirements for time to be spent on each subject.

— Make several copies of your weekly schedule planning form.

— Place lunch and recess, special classes, and pullout program times on a copy of the form.

— Think about how you would like to begin the day.

— Think about what type of activity would be appropriate right after lunch.

— Think about how you would like to end the day.

— Begin placing subjects at appropriate places in the schedule.

— Recheck the minutes of instruction you have scheduled against any state or district requirements.

— Get feedback on your plan. Adjust it as needed throughout the year.

— Use your weekly schedule to create a generic frame for your daily lesson plans (see page 100).

TIME	MONDAY	TUESDAY	WEDNESDAY	THURSDAY	FRIDAY
8:50–9:15	Opening and Sharing	Opening and Sharing	Opening and Sharing	Opening and Sharing	Opening and Sharing
9:15–9:45	Whole Group Phonics/Spelling	Whole Group Phonics/Spelling	Whole Group Phonics/Spelling	Whole Group Phonics/Spelling	Whole Group Phonics/Spelling
9:45–10:15	Whole Group Reading/Writing	Whole Group Reading/Writing	Whole Group Reading/Writing	Whole Group Reading/Writing	Whole Group Reading/Writing
10:15–10:30	BREAK	BREAK	BREAK	BREAK	BREAK
10:30–10:45	Reading Grp. #1 + Seatwork/Centers	Reading Grp. #1 + Seatwork/Centers	Reading Grp. #1 + Seatwork/Centers	Reading Grp. #1 + Seatwork/Centers	Reading Grp. #1 + Seatwork/Centers
10:45–11:00	Reading Grp. #2 + Seatwork/Centers	Reading Grp. #2 + Seatwork/Centers	Reading Grp. #2 + Seatwork/Centers	Reading Grp. #2 + Seatwork/Centers	Reading Grp. #2 + Seatwork/Centers
11:00–11:15	Reading Grp. #3 + Seatwork/Centers	Reading Grp. #3 + Seatwork/Centers	Reading Grp. #3 + Seatwork/Centers	Reading Grp. #3 + Seatwork/Centers	Reading Grp. #3 + Seatwork/Centers
11:15–12:20	Math	Math	Math	Math	Math
12:20–1:00	LUNCH	LUNCH	LUNCH	LUNCH	LUNCH
	1:00–1:10 Story Time	1:00–1:10 Story Time	1:00–1:20 Story Time	1:00–1:10 Story Time	1:00–1:10 Story Time
	1:10–2:00 Social Studies	1:10–2:05 Science	1:20–2:00 LIBRARY	1:10–1:55 ART	1:10–1:50 S.S./Sci./Health
	2:00–2:45 MUSIC	2:05–2:45 P.E.	2:00–2:45 Health	1:55–2:05 Housecleaning	1:50–2:05 Friday Special
	2:45–2:50 Clean/Dismiss	2:45–2:50 Clean/Dismiss	2:45–2:50 Clean/Dismiss	2:05–2:50 P.E./Dismiss	2:05–2:50 P.E./Dismiss

☼ I scattered potentially active subjects, like science and centers, throughout the day to break up more sedentary subjects like writing.

☼ If some of my students left the room for more help in reading, I tried to coordinate that time to be during reading activities rather than math, as those students were expected to be in my classroom for math instruction.

Try your schedule for instruction for two weeks before adjusting it.

TIME	MONDAY	TUESDAY	WEDNESDAY	THURSDAY	FRIDAY
9:00	Opening/Job/ Silent Reading Calendars/Life Skill	8:55–9:30 Opening/Reading/ Calendar	8:55–9:30 Opening/Reading	8:55–9:30 Opening/Reading/ Calendar	8:55–9:55 Opening/P.E.
10:00	10:00–10:45 Math	9:30–10:45 Math/Science	9:30–12:35 Primary Multiage Cooperative Learning Thematic Explorations	9:30–10:50 Math/Science	9:55–10:45 Spelling/Calendar
11:00	10:45–11:15 Literacy Workshop	10:45–11:15 Literacy Workshop		10:50–11:40 ART	10:45–1:15 Literacy Workshop
12:00	11:15–12:15 Integrated Thematic Instruction	11:15–12:15 Integrated Thematic Instruction		11:40–12:15 Spelling/Writing	11:15–12:15 Integrated Thematic Instruction
	12:15–12:35 Novel	12:15–12:35 Novel		12:15–12:35 Novel	12:15–12:35 Novel
1:00	12:35–1:10 LUNCH	12:35–1:10 LUNCH	12:35–1:10 LUNCH	12:35–1:10 LUNCH	12:35–1:10 LUNCH
2:00	1:10–1:55 Spelling/Writing	1:10–1:40 Writing	1:10–1:50 Writing/Thematic Extensions	1:10–1:40 Writing	1:10–1:40 Writing
	1:55–2:45 LIBRARY	1:40–2:15 Int. Them. Instr.	1:50–2:40 COMPUTER	1:40–2:10 Sharing/Banking	1:40–2:00 Wrap-Up
3:00	2:45–3:11 Cleanup/ Ask Me About/ Celebration	2:15–3:11 Cleanup/ MUSIC/Dismiss	2:40–3:11 Calendar/Cleanup	2:10–3:00 P.E. 3:00–3:11 Cleanup	2:00–3:05 Jacobsonville 3:05–3:11 Cleanup

Daily Lesson Plans

Before you tackle the lesson-plan book, let's think about all the components that need to be considered as you begin planning a lesson. I'm certain that you had plenty of practice writing complete lessons during your teacher preparation. The organizer below is simply a reminder of the process, a "think-aloud" to ensure that all of your lessons are high-quality learning experiences. At the beginning, you may need to refer to these questions frequently, but rest assured that after several months of planning on a daily basis, the process will become a habit for you.

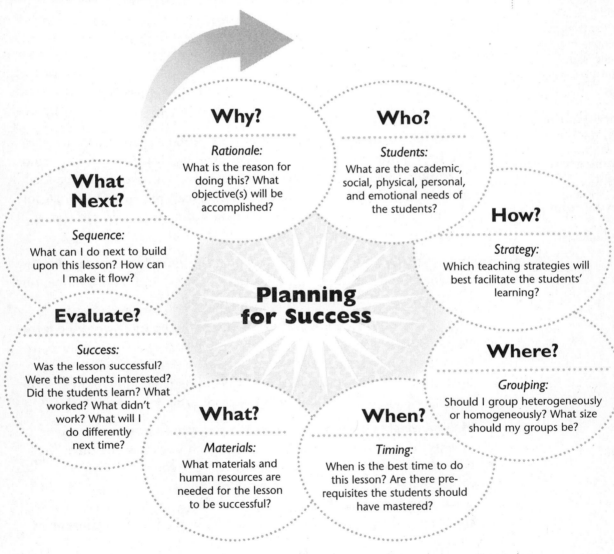

Why?

Rationale:
What is the reason for doing this? What objective(s) will be accomplished?

Who?

Students:
What are the academic, social, physical, personal, and emotional needs of the students?

What Next?

Sequence:
What can I do next to build upon this lesson? How can I make it flow?

How?

Strategy:
Which teaching strategies will best facilitate the students' learning?

Planning for Success

Evaluate?

Success:
Was the lesson successful? Were the students interested? Did the students learn? What worked? What didn't work? What will I do differently next time?

Where?

Grouping:
Should I group heterogeneously or homogeneously? What size should my groups be?

What?

Materials:
What materials and human resources are needed for the lesson to be successful?

When?

Timing
When is the best time to do this lesson? Are there prerequisites the students should have mastered?

Isn't it amazing how many things a teacher has to think about to plan just one lesson? And that's not all! The lesson plan has to be presented in a format that is approved by the site administrator. So, let's move on to daily lesson plans.

Daily lesson plans detail specific activities and content that will be taught during a particular week. They usually include the objectives you will be teaching that week, procedures for delivering instruction and assessing the students, student groupings, and materials you will need to carry out the plans successfully. As with all planning, the format of lesson plans will vary from school to school. Many school districts provide lesson-plan books, while others allow teachers to develop their own format. Using a computer to generate plan forms facilitates the process. While there are programs designed specifically for writing lesson plans, you can also use a word-processing program and create a scripted plan or one using a table.

Actual lesson plans can be highly structured and linear or laid out like a web. Some teachers show minute-by-minute details of when and how activities will occur; others show the overall plan for the whole week to create a more flexible structure. Regardless of how your principal prefers your plans to be structured, below are some general suggestions for successful lesson planning:

☼ **Your lesson plans should be readable and detailed** enough that a substitute teacher could teach from them in an emergency.

☼ **Consider making a copy or two of each week's plan.** I used to take one copy home and place others at key areas in my classroom so I could leave my actual lesson-plan book on my desk at all times, available for the principal. This also assisted me at home with preparing materials for upcoming lessons and planning for the following week without fear of misplacing my plan book!

☼ **Try scripting your lessons.** It was time-consuming, but in my first few years of teaching it helped me be better organized and more confident in front of my students. (See sample on page 58.)

☼ As a general rule, **begin working on plans for the next week no later than Thursday**. By then you will have an idea of which lessons weren't completed, the objectives that need to be reinforced, and which upcoming schoolwide activities need to be integrated into your plan. If you leave planning until Friday after school, it may not get done!

☼ **Make a master copy of the planning pages you use**, and write or type in those activities that stay the same each week and the times they occur (you could also make a template on your computer if your principal agrees). *Make several copies of the new pages to replace the blank lesson-plan pages*, but don't copy them too far in advance, in case you change your weekly schedule. Then just fill in the blanks on the copies with specifics for the week.

☼ **Balance grouping strategies and activities** in each learning style or intelligence so you are meeting the needs of all your students.

☼ **Check with your principal for guidelines** on when he or she will want to look at your plans. Some principals make a point of viewing new teachers' lesson plans on a weekly basis so they can provide on-the-spot assistance throughout the school year.

Monday	**8:50–9:10** **Opening**—(attendance, lunch count, singing, sharing, pledge, song, 30 seconds of silence) Students to share today: _____ _____ **9:10–9:20** **Calendar**—	**9:20–9:35** **Read Aloud**— **9:35–9:45** **Journaling**— **9:45–9:55** **Read With Partner**—	**9:55–10:30** **Shared Reading**— **Response**—

Page 106 shows an example of traditional plans; refer to page 58 for an example of scripted plans. These plans are not necessarily model plans; rather, they show a variety of planning formats.

Planning for a Substitute Teacher

The worst things happen when we're not prepared! As a brand-new teacher, the last thing I expected was to be called for a week of jury duty at the end of November when I had several involved projects going on—preparing to celebrate Thanksgiving as well as the winter holiday festivities. Because I had not prepared generic plans for a substitute teacher to use, I had to work late every night after coming home from jury duty to write substitute plans and prepare materials, then drive by school the next morning to drop them off before returning to the courthouse. I was a wreck, the substitute was nervous, and my students were confused by the last-minute changes to our normal routine.

From then on, I kept a notebook or folder for substitute teachers in plain sight on my desk. It contained information on my classroom management practices, my students, and my expectations. When I knew I was going to be absent, I wrote out detailed lesson plans and referred the substitute to the notebook. For those times when I did not know I was going to be out, I created generic lesson plans; these will be described later.

Include the following information in your substitute teacher notebook or folder:

You say you're not going to get sick... but just in case, get your substitute notebook or folder and plans ready! Schools are breeding grounds for germs, and you know how sharing children are!

Yes, I'm back! And that means that it's time to talk to a peer about substitute teacher plans. What does your school require? Where can you see some samples? Have an actual substitute look at your notebook or folder and plans to get a realistic view of their effectiveness.

Behavior management system—Describe how you manage student behavior. Don't forget to have management items, such as tokens, stickers, chance slips, or Behavior Bucks, available if you want the substitute to use your system.

Rules and procedures—Take time to describe how you expect procedures to be carried out in your classroom. Try making a cassette tape describing your procedures, sharing special instructions for the day or even giving a verbal tour of your classroom. Punch out the tabs so the tape can't be accidentally erased, and leave it in a tape player on your desk with instructions for the substitute. It really simplifies the process of explaining class routines!

Emergency procedures—Keep information on fire drills, shelter-in-place, lockdown, missing child, and other possible emergencies handy. Have all emergency materials (*current* class list for fire drill, first-aid kit, health office passes) easily accessible.

Schedule for instruction—Provide the substitute with a *current* copy of your schedule. Make note of any pullout classes (reading improvement, GATE, speech, resource room) and which students attend them. Let the substitute know if special education teachers come to your classroom rather than pulling the children out of class.

Class list and seating chart—Include a *current* copy of your class list and seating chart. Consider making an extra copy of the seating chart and asking the substitute to make notes about behavior, who read, who had problems with math, and so forth, directly on the copy. It's a great reference for you and will help the substitute get to know your students better as he or she observes them throughout the day.

Lesson plans—I've found the quickest way to prepare lesson plans for substitutes is to determine strategies that would work with any content and then create detailed, but generic, lesson plans for each day of the week that are easily implemented. I made sure my plans for each day had a thorough explanation of the day's regular routines, including lunch and specialists' classes. Then I had a different math lesson in each plan: Monday—review addition sheet and directions for practicing addition flash cards; Tuesday—review sheet on subtraction and directions for using the math storyboards; Wednesday—whole-group review of story problems and directions for creating story problems in pairs to exchange with another pair; Thursday—"Telling Time" Bingo and individual practice on telling-time review sheet; Friday—directions for playing Math Jeopardy. I also included literacy strategies to be used with whatever story or article was currently being read in class: Monday—Venn diagram; Tuesday—story web; Wednesday—letter to the teacher; Thursday—mind map; Friday—write a summary of the week's readings.

I also included generic science and social studies lessons that could be easily implemented. I kept fully stocked folders of handouts and other materials for each day of the week, so that if I was absent on any Monday of the year, the generic Monday plan supplanted my real lesson plans for the day and the materials were readily available. These plans were easy for a substitute to follow, and when I returned to school, I got to teach my real lesson plans the way I had intended.

Student helpers—Indicate which students the substitute should call on for help. If you have a student helper program in your class, let the substitute know that you expect the students to handle their jobs just as if you were there. Train student helpers thoroughly to ensure quality work whenever you're absent.

Special-needs students—Students with special needs often have difficulty dealing with their teacher's absence. Prepare the substitute with the names of students who might have a strong reaction or who might need extra help. Include a description of what usually works to help the student get through the problem with a minimum of disruption. Make the substitute aware of any staff members who can assist him or her in case of an emergency.

Teaching materials and teacher's guides—Even though you may be comfortable not using teacher's guides for instruction, have them available in case you need to call in a substitute at the last minute. A teacher's guide may be helpful if you lack the time to prepare detailed substitute plans.

Prepare the substitute—If possible, prepare the substitute prior to your absence by letting him or her know what grade you teach, if you have duty, if there is a field trip or other special event that day, and what social studies or science content should be taught.

Prepare the students—If you know that you will be absent ahead of time, let your students know that you will be gone, who will be taking your place, what you have planned for the day, and how you expect them to behave. It will be easier for the substitute to teach and handle students if they are not surprised by your absence.

The following pages include one section of a sample generic lesson plan and a sample Substitute Information Sheet.

Sample Lesson Plan—Traditional Format

* OPENING = ATTENDANCE, LUNCH COUNT, PLEDGE, SONG, 30 SECONDS OF SILENCE, CALENDAR   ** BREAK = SNACK, RESTROOM, DRINKS

	Whole-Group Reading/Language	Small-Group Reading/Language Reinforcement and Development	Mathematics	Lunch	Integrated Subjects
MONDAY	8:50–9:10 OPENING* 9:10–9:40 PHONICS OBJ: L 3.1, R 21 PLAN: ◆ Shared read, *The Jigaree* ◆ ID unknown words ◆ Review story pattern ◆ Give seat-work directions for drawing a Jigaree and extending story 9:40–10:05 RDG/LANG OBJ: R 1.6, 2.1, 1.1 PLAN: ◆ Intro. "not" and "for"; use in content ◆ Present rhyming long vowel sounds ◆ Brainstorm likenesses and differences of rhyming words in *The Jigaree* ◆ Define "rhyming"	10:05–10:20 D—READING ◆ Choose group name ◆ Look through *Mooncake*; predict content; take books to desk for free time A/C—WRITING B—Seat-work 10:20–10:30 BREAK** 10:30–10:45 A—READING ◆ Choose group name ◆ Look through *Little Bear*; predict content; take books to desk for free time B—CENTERS C/D—SEATWORK 10:45–11:00 B—READING ◆ Choose group name ◆ Look through *Bear Facts*; predict content; take books to desk for free time C/D—CENTERS A—SEATWORK 11:00–11:15 C—READING ◆ Choose group name ◆ Look through *Bears*; predict content; take books to desk for free time A—CENTERS B/D—WRITING	11:15–12:20 OBJ: M 1.6, 1.5—Patterns PLAN: ◆ Free exploration of pattern blocks ◆ Finish patterns started on OHP, have students create patterns on OHP for class to finish ◆ Use pattern cards at desks 12:15–12:30 PREP. FOR LUNCH; FINISH MATH	LUNCH 12:20–1:00	1:00–1:10 STORY/FILM *Chicken Soup with Rice*—Sendak 1:10–2:00 HEALTH/SCIENCE/S.S. OBJ: Months, autumn PLAN: ◆ Review months from story ◆ List/group/label months into seasons ◆ Brainstorm what happens in the autumn ◆ Show filmstrip *Fall into Winter* ◆ Remind students to collect leaves for tomorrow 2:00–2:45 MUSIC
TUESDAY	8:50–9:10 OPENING* 9:10–9:40 PHONICS OBJ: R 1.5 PLAN: ◆ Review long "a" ◆ Intro. short "a" ◆ Discuss short "a" pictures ◆ Brainstorm short "a" words ◆ Give seat-work directions to make short "a" apple word wheel 9:40–10:05 RDG/LANG OBJ: R 2.1, 1.6, 1.1 PLAN: ◆ Intro. "at" and "with"; use in content ◆ Teach and practice definition of rhyming ◆ Brainstorm long vowel rhyming pairs ◆ Write a 2-line rhyme; illustrate	10:05–10:20 D—READING ◆ Model read, *Mooncake* ◆ Review vocabulary cards ◆ List and discuss unknown vocab.; make word cards for story words A/C—PAIRED RDG. B—SEATWORK 10:20–10:30 BREAK** 10:30–10:45 A—READING ◆ Paired read, *Little Bear* ◆ List and discuss unknown vocab; add words to personal picture dictionary B—CENTERS C/D—SEATWORK 10:45–11:00 B—READING ◆ Model read, *Bear Facts* ◆ List and discuss unknown vocab; create glossary C/D—CENTERS A—SEATWORK 11:00–11:15 C—READING ◆ Model read, *Bears* ◆ List and discuss unknown vocab.; make word cards for story vocab. A—CENTERS B/D—PAIRED RDG.	11:15–12:20 OBJ: M 1.6, 1.5—Patterns PLAN: ◆ Introduce AB patterns with pattern blocks ◆ Make AB patterns on OHP ◆ Make as many AB patterns at desk as possible using pattern blocks; record patterns on grid paper; compare with a partner 12:15–12:20 PREP. FOR LUNCH; FINISH MATH	LUNCH 12:20–1:00	1:00–1:10 STORY/FILM *Chicken Tricks*—Lloyd 1:10–2:05 HEALTH/SCIENCE/S.S OBJ: Sci.2.2—Months, autumn PLAN: ◆ Review months with knuckle calendar ◆ Make list of autumn things ◆ Use Venn diagram to compare and contrast leaves ◆ Make Leaf People art project 2:05–2:45 P.E.

Sample Substitute Information Sheet

◆ **Opening Procedures** (lunch count, attendance, chores, and so on): Pick up students at 9:00 on line "17" outside. See lunch folder on my desk for lunch count details. Attendance folder is red; I keep it hanging on the door. Take attendance in the morning and again after lunch. Student "messenger" will take folder to the office after lunch.

◆ **Lunch** (time, duty; do you eat with students?): Lunch is 12:20–1:00. There is a line for hot lunch and a line for cold lunch. Early duty if from 12:20–12:50 in the lunchroom. Late duty is from 12:50–1:00 on the playground. You eat in the teacher's lounge.

◆ **Dismissal** (exact time; are buses involved?): Dismissal bell rings at 3:16. We do have buses, so students need to be out of the room no later than the second bell at 3:21. Students need to get their "mail" and put up their chairs.

◆ **Fire Drill** (Where does the class report? How do they get there?): My class goes straight out to the playground and lines up on the grass. Take emergency folder with you, turn off the lights, and close the door. Keep students quiet outside.

◆ **Discipline** (What are your discipline, intervention, or behavior modification procedures?): Give chance slips to students who are behaving appropriately—be generous! They will keep them at their desks until I return. If you need assistance with serious behaviors, contact Mrs. Smith in Room 19. Send students to the office with a written report only in emergency.

◆ **Privileges**

Restroom: Child stands by door. You nod "yes" or "no." One child at a time.

Drinking Fountain: I allow students to get drinks whenever I am not teaching the whole group.

Library: Up to three students may visit the school library during the last 20 minutes of each day if their work is done.

Other: Helpers—chart is hanging by the back chalkboard and the coat hook. Use the helpers often; they know their jobs well.

◆ **Other Procedures**

Student Illness: Send student to the office with a written health slip. Health slips are in my top right-hand desk drawer.

Rainy Days: Coordinate recess with Mrs. Smith, Room 19.

Class Signals (voice, lights, other techniques): Raise hand, ring chimes, clap rhythm for kids to repeat; continue speaking when they're quiet.

Free-Time Activities: After reading seat work is finished, students go to centers (see chart in front of room). After math, students may get their cubes or a chalkboard to practice math. Students may read or write at any time.

Name of Parents or Other Helpers and Their Duties: Mrs. Wellman, Monday 10:30–11:15; Mrs. West, Wednesday, 10:30–11:15; Mr. Hughes, Friday, 10:30–11:15. These parents help children with writing. They know what to do.

What do you expect from a substitute teacher? Follow lesson plans as closely as possible. Emphasize the positive and ignore the negative. Collect student work from their folders at the end of the day and place on my desk. Make sure chairs are up and floor is clean. Check with the office before leaving to see if you are needed for the following day.

◆ **Breaks for Snack, Bathroom, and Drinks:** Mornings, 10:20–10:30; Afternoon, 12:30–1:00.

◆ **Where to Find:**

Teacher Editions of Texts: above red basket stand to the left of my desk

Lesson Plans: my desk

Extra Pencils and Crayons: pencils—in student boxes; crayons, markers, rulers—on round table

AV Equipment: behind my desk

Class List(s): Red attendance folder on desk or lunch-count chart in lunch folder.

Emergency Procedures: folder, map, tape for shelter-in-place drill and other emergencies is hanging on the door.

◆ **Children With Special Needs (physical, emotion, medical):** Chris sometimes acts out physically; don't let him get frustrated. Allow Katie to help Susan during reading and writing. Send Jeff to the nurse's office after lunch for medication.

◆ **Children Who Go to Special Classes and Times:** Chris and Susan—Resource Room, every day, 9:15–12:00; Stephen, Katie, Karyn, Jeffrey, and Edward—GATE, M, T, Th, 11:00-11:45; Jennifer—RIP, teacher comes to room.

◆ **Additional Information or Instructions:** My students are in numbered groups. It is helpful to call them by groups when lining up, coming to the front for instruction, and so on. Walk students to music, PE, library, and lunch as scheduled. You are free to return to the classroom or visit the teacher's lounge during special classes.

One of the greatest proactive management techniques lies in the quality of classroom instruction. Think about a class you've taken that was interesting, that involved you, that had variety, that met your needs, and that was meaningful. Did you whisper or pass notes? Did you neglect your homework? Did you resent the teacher? Probably not! Contrast this with a class that was boring, non-interactive, not individualized, and irrelevant. It is possible that your behavior might have been different in this scenario. This section addresses ways to plan for and implement good instruction and will be useful for improving student behavior as well as student learning.

Beginning-of-the-Year Assessments

During the first couple of weeks, use a variety of baseline assessments to determine where your students are so you will be able to plan appropriate instruction and measure progress during the year. Watch your students carefully in varied situations (during instruction, on the playground, in line, working in groups). Practicing "with-it-ness" (being continually aware of what is going on with students) will help you learn about your students' strengths and needs—academically, behaviorally, and socially. While you don't want to overwhelm students with assessments on the first few days, you should be able to work some of the following into your schedule:

- ☼ **Interest Inventory and/or Attitude Survey** (see pages 170–173)—Assess the interests of your students. Each child can be a "specialist" on some topic and a resource for other students looking for information in that area.

- ☼ **Reading**—Try the San Diego Quick Assessment, Frye's Word List, an informal reading inventory, and oral reading.

- ☼ **Writing**—Assign an informal writing sample on a topic of student's choice or a student analysis of a piece of writing.

- ☼ **Spelling**—Assign a five-minute word write, spelling dictation task, or Qualitative Spelling Inventory.

- ☼ **Math**—Try problem solving with journaling (students describe how they solved the problem), or have them write everything they know about adding, subtracting, multiplying, dividing, telling time, and counting money.

Some of your most useful information will come from observing your students and asking them questions about their thinking. The following list of specific things to notice was adapted from two excellent sources: *A Kid-Watching Guide: Evaluation for Whole Language Classrooms* by TAWL (Tusconans Applying Whole Language), January 1984, No. 9, and *Assessment Alternatives in Mathematics* by the California Mathematics Council.

For more information on assessment, flip ahead to page 150.

Check with teachers at your building to find out which assessments and tests are used at your school. They may even share copies of some assessments that are just right for your students.

Observing and Questioning Children

OBSERVATIONS

Behavior...

- ✷ Does the child appear confident?
- ✷ Does the child make eye contact?
- ✷ Does the child demonstrate self-control?
- ✷ Does the child follow teacher requests?

Work Habits...

- ✷ Does the child show initiative?
- ✷ Does the child stay focused on tasks?
- ✷ Does the child complete tasks on time?
- ✷ Does the child do neat and careful work?

Organization...

- ✷ Does the child keep track of supplies?
- ✷ How is the child's desk maintained?
- ✷ Is the child able to follow your directions?

Communication...

- ✷ Does the child speak in complete sentences?
- ✷ Does the child carry on informal conversations with other students?
- ✷ Does the child demonstrate characteristics of active listening?

Cooperation...

- ✷ Does the child work productively with others in a group?
- ✷ Is the child able to solve social problems without intervention by the teacher?
- ✷ Does the child tend to interact with peers, older children, younger children, or adults at recess?
- ✷ Does the child respond in a positive manner to requests from peers?

QUESTIONS

Behavior...

- ✷ What makes it easy or hard for you to follow rules?
- ✷ How do you make good behavior choices in school?

Work Habits...

- ✷ Was it hard for you to start or finish the task?
- ✷ Did it take you longer to do this task than you thought it would?
- ✷ How do you keep your mind on your work with other people around you?
- ✷ Did you do your personal best?

Organization...

- ✷ Do you have a place to keep your backpack and homework at home?
- ✷ Explain how you organized your desk.
- ✷ Tell me what you were thinking when you started this task.

Communication...

- ✷ Would you please say that again more clearly and completely?
- ✷ Do you like to talk to your friends?
- ✷ What does it look like and sound like when people are listening?

Cooperation...

- ✷ What did you do at recess today?
- ✷ How did you work out your problem with ____?
- ✷ Did you work as hard on the project as the other students in your group?
- ✷ Would you rather work with a group or by yourself?

Effective Instruction

Setting the Stage

You planned a wonderful lesson. You had all the resources and materials ready. You knew exactly what you expected from the students. So why didn't it go as well as you had planned? Let's look at the first characteristic of quality lessons, setting the stage for instruction, to learn how an effective teacher creates "magic" in the classroom.

First, recognize that you must have your students' full attention. I very rarely teach an important concept while the students are at their desks. To minimize distractions, I invite students to sit on the floor in one part of the room. Remember that proximity is a good management tool. Being close to the students helps you maintain eye contact and notice off-task behavior immediately.

My procedure for coming to the whole-group instruction area is "leave everything at your desk, stand up, walk softly to the front of the room, find a place where you can learn, and sit down with your legs crossed." Every time I need the whole class to come to the group area, I have one student model that procedure; then I call one group at a time to the front, asking them to copy the procedure as modeled. It takes a few seconds, but eliminates a mad rush. Remember to offer verbal feedback as students are going through any of your class procedures to reinforce appropriate behavior.

Once the class is gathered in the whole-group instruction area, you must get them to focus on you. If students are talking, quarreling, or playing while you teach, they won't learn the lesson. Before teaching anything, make sure that all students are with you by having a pre-arranged signal (music box, chimes, rain stick, raised hand, clapping pattern). Other great attention-getters include a whisper, a character voice, an animated expression or a call-and-response chant: "Body still. Arms folded. Eyes forward. Ears listening. Lips quiet." These procedures must be taught and reinforced often, or they won't become a routine for the students. Don't start teaching until all eyes are on you; you'll have to teach students what listening "looks like, sounds like, and feels like" in your classroom.

One of the scariest things to do as a new teacher is to wait until students are ready. As you wait for attention, notice which students are ready for the lesson and thank them ("I'm going to wait until everyone is ready to learn. Tap the top of your head if you're ready—yes, I see that you are ready, John."). Waiting can be effective if the students know that you have something to say and that your lesson will be interesting.

Once you have the students' attention, don't risk losing it by not being ready to teach. Have all your materials laid out close at hand. Have a copy of the lesson plan where you can refer to it. Know what you expect from the students in terms of behavior and academics. If you ask for students' attention, then walk over to your desk to get the materials for the lesson, they may learn that it's not important for them to listen when you ask them to do so.

Introducing the Lesson

Get the students excited about the lesson by arousing their curiosity. Try these techniques:

Lower your voice and let them in on a "big secret."	*"Wow! Do I have big news for you! Did you know that yesterday the best weatherman in the world made an announcement? Who has seen a weatherman on the news?..."*
Tell them a personal story about how what you will be studying relates to your life.	*"Yesterday morning, I took a walk in the desert. While I was out walking, I remembered that it was Groundhog Day. I came across a burrow that looked too big for a ground squirrel...."*
Show them actual objects or photos of the topic.	*"Here is a picture of a shadow all by itself. Can anyone guess what kind of animal/object is making the shadow?..."*
Read them a children's book or sing a song related to the topic.	*"Me and my shadow...."*
Relate the topic to something else you have studied.	*"Remember last month when we studied weather? Who can share something we learned about the sun and types of weather?..."*

Students pay attention only to what they want to hear about. It's the teacher's job to make learning so exciting that students can't help but want to be involved in the lesson.

Remember that you can only lecture for a short time (kindergarten—up to 5 minutes; fourth grade—up to 12 minutes) before students start to "check out" of the lecture. To maintain their attention, use a mix of the following strategies:

☼ Ask questions along the way.

☼ Break into song.

☼ Ask students to demonstrate the concept being learned for the class.

☼ Have them vote with thumbs up or down.

☼ Have them close their eyes and imagine the concept using all their senses.

☼ Create a chant for the concept ("Shadow, shadow, you're following me. Shadow, shadow, how big can you be? In the morning you're big

St. Patrick's Day was always a fun day for my primary students. Here, we are looking for the leprechaun in a paper bag that was "magically" moving and rustling!

and tall. At noon, you're very small. At night, you're not there at all. Shadow, shadow, come play with me.").

If students are not somehow involved in the lesson, they probably won't gain a good understanding of the concept you are teaching.

Teaching the Lesson

It's important to know precisely what you're teaching and why you're teaching it. Then, communicate it clearly to students in simple, everyday language. Break the lesson into comprehensible chunks, making sure students are paying attention when you speak. Check to see if your students comprehend the concepts by informally assessing their understanding at frequent points in the lesson—thumbs up or thumbs down; echoing the teacher; practicing the information in a meaningful way. Teachers can get so caught up the act of teaching, we forget to check if the students are learning!

Sometimes you will tell students what the objective of the lesson is: "Today we're going to be learning about geology. Does anyone know what geology is? Geology is the study of rocks. In this lesson, you will learn about the properties of rocks. Properties are general characteristics of rocks, like hardness, luster, and color...."

At other times, you will want students to build the objective for themselves through exploration: "Here is a box of rocks. Use your senses to help you describe them for me; I'll write down what you say. George said, 'Rocks are lots of colors.' Mary said, 'Some rocks are hard.' Andy said, 'Some rocks are shiny and some are dull.' Sally said, 'Rocks are different sizes.' Students, you have just described some of the properties of rocks. What do you think I mean by 'properties'? Look at what I've written as you shared your ideas...."

Ask the students why it might be important to learn about the topic you're teaching. Get them to stretch beyond, "I'll need to know it when I grow up." Help them develop an understanding of how the objective relates to their lives now. "Today we're going to practice making change. When you go to the store next time, you'll be able to make sure that the clerk gives you the correct change." Sometimes a real-life application of the content will be elusive. Model the joy of learning for learning's sake for those hard-to-apply skills and concepts: "Wow! I never knew that! What an awesome thing to know."

Remind students of the purpose of the task throughout the lesson. While you want to honor "teachable" moments and be flexible enough to capitalize on the needs and interests of the students, make sure that they remain focused on the lesson you intended to teach. If you get distracted by an important side issue, come back to the main topic after the side issue is adequately processed.

Using Effective Teaching Strategies

Effective lessons provide students with meaningful experiences to help them master the content of the lesson. When I look at my curriculum, I see so many skills that need to be taught during the course of the year that it's tempting to rush through them to cover them all. Instead, we need to "uncover the curriculum" by involving our students in the process of learning. When the learner feels in control, higher-level learning is possible. Recent findings support the constructivist model of learning, which proposes that learners must invest in their own learning, connect current information with prior knowledge, learn skills and concepts in depth, and relate new knowledge to the real world. Facilitating to help students get beneath the surface of a skill or concept may appear to take more time; however, the payoff is greater understanding of the content and retention of the knowledge beyond the test.

To help students delve into content, vary your instructional methods to meet the learning styles of all students and give them many opportunities to work with new material in different contexts. For example, if you are studying reptiles, see if you can get a discount at a pet shop so you can purchase a small snake or lizard for the students to observe. Get as many books, films, and filmstrips on reptiles as possible. Have the students do a K-W-L on reptiles (see page 144), draw a picture of a reptile and label the parts, create a reptile-habitat diorama, research two reptiles and compare and contrast them, create a play about a reptile, write a letter to find out which reptiles are endangered, and so on. Do some activities individually and others in small groups or as a whole group. Offer students some choices about which learning activities to do.

I am a firm believer that students must be involved in the lesson. You cannot learn to swim by hearing a lecture. You cannot understand the mysteries of the desert without experiencing it yourself. To assist students in constructing their own understanding, teachers must learn to ask and answer questions. Questioning is an art that requires plenty of practice.

Remember Bloom's taxonomy? Take another look at Bloom's ideas for moving beyond knowledge and comprehension questions and activities. Teach students about different types of questions they can ask, and give them opportunities to practice asking questions in addition to answering them. An exceptional teacher shared a winning idea with me: she wrote a variety of questions at different levels on sentence strips, then placed them high on the walls around her room. When she needed a good question, all she had to do was look around!

The following information on answering and asking questions was adapted from the Honolulu Community College Faculty Development Web site (www.hcc.hawaii.edu/education/hcc/facdev/askquest.html). When students ask you a question, it is tempting to simply tell them the answer; however, students can learn more if you use one of the first six options below before directly answering the question. Let's use "Why are some rocks red and others gray?" as a sample question.

" *The important thing is to never stop questioning!* "

—*Albert Einstein*

I recently visited an Internet site on questioning: **www.oir.uiuc.edu/did /booklets/question /question.html**. It is a helpful tutorial on questioning skills.

☼ **Repeat the question, clarifying**—"Are you asking about the rocks at Red Rock Canyon?"

☼ **Redirect the question**—"Does anyone have any information on how rocks get their color?"

☼ **Ask probing questions**—"What do you know about things changing color? Do you remember the experiment where we put a white carnation in water dyed green? What happened to the carnation? What things other than dye cause changes in colors?"

☼ **Promote a discussion among the students**—"Let's make some guesses about why the rocks are different colors. I'll record your thoughts on the chalkboard. Who has some ideas for Tony?"

☼ **Postpone answering the question**—"We are going to do an experiment on rocks this Friday. I think after you explore a bit, you'll have some more ideas."

☼ **Admit when you do not know an answer**—"I don't know. Let's find out together. How might we find the answer?"

☼ **Directly answer the question**—"The red-colored rocks are sandstone. They are made from bits of sand that has been naturally cemented together. Scientists believe that the red is caused from bits of iron that was deposited along with the sand. The gray-colored rocks are limestone. They are made from bits of rocks and shells that cement at the bottom of the sea or ocean and keep their grayish-white color."

Answer students' questions in a variety of ways. Avoid consistently telling the answers; students need to think about the material to construct their own understanding.

Giving Directions

One essential skill for effective teaching is knowing how to give directions. You must clearly convey two messages to your students: "This is what you're going to do" and "This is what's expected of you while you do it." To give good directions, follow these three steps:

1. Define what students will do and how they will do it.

2. Decide how much information your students can handle at once.

3. Determine the most effective method for delivering the set of directions.

A lesson I quickly learned my first year of teaching was to keep directions simple, model them, and have the students repeat them or act them out before performing the task. It takes a few extra moments, but it helps your students remember what to do when they're on their own. Here is an example of thorough directions for a fairly complex primary task:

You are going to work at your desk. You will need scissors and glue. What will you need?... First, write your name on your paper. Here is my paper; help me spell my name at the top.... Second, cut out the duck; take your time as you cut so you have smooth cuts like this. (Demonstrate.) Third, write the word yellow *two times. (Demonstrate.) Fourth, use two drops of glue to fasten the wing feather to the duck. What happens if I use more than two drops?... Use two drops of glue to fasten the word* yellow *to the duck. (Demonstrate.) Fifth, throw away your scraps, close your glue, put away your glue and scissors, and place your duck on the project table. Watch as I do the cleanup procedure. (Demonstrate.) Now, let's go back and make sure that everyone knows what to do. I'll write the steps for the project on the board. Joey, what is the first thing you will do?... No, before you cut you have to do something else really important.... Yes, write your name. Sue, what is the second thing you will do?... Yes, cut out the duck. Sarah, what is the third thing you will do?...Yes, write the word* yellow. *How many times?... Yes, Ruby, two times.... John, tell us the fourth thing we'll have to do.... Yes, and remember to be careful with your glue. And finally, what happens fifth, Danny?... Cleanup time! Now, what should you do if you forget what comes next while you're working?... I'm glad you remembered that, George—look back at the board where I just wrote the directions. Are you ready?... Okay, green group, go back to your desks; everyone watch the green group to see how they walk back. Wow! They aren't even talking. Super!*

Students Who Finish Early

Nothing is more frustrating to students than being either the first *or* the last one finished with an assignment. Minimizing the number of problems you expect your students to complete may help lessen the time you need to provide extra activities for students who finish early. I remember as a student finishing assignments early only to have the teacher add on more problems. With that response, why would anyone want to work hard? I also remember not being allowed to participate in a special activity because I was having trouble finishing an assignment. If students do finish early, I like to give them choices of enrichment activities that are rewarding to them without seeming to punish those who need more time on the assignment. Because most of my lessons are built around science and social studies concepts, researching a topic is always an option, as is writing, reading, and making up math problems. Many children enjoy helping other students and the teacher, but be careful of overusing any one student's learning time on non-instructional activities.

❋ **Tip** ❋

Giving Good Directions

◆ Get their attention before giving directions by clapping, using chimes, or saying, "If you're listening, tap the top of your head; if you're listening, pat your stomach; if you're listening, sit up straight."

◆ Create a "giving directions" procedure like "Stop, fold your hands, close your lips, look at the teacher, open your ears."

◆ Break directions for primary students into small chunks and have students repeat the directions and/or model them for the rest of the class.

◆ Write complicated directions on the board, perhaps with representative pictures, so students can refer to the board instead of interrupting your teaching.

◆ Tape-record complicated directions and place them on the cassette player at a listening center so students have immediate access to the directions.

◆ Teach your students that they must quietly ask the others at their table for information on the directions before coming to you. ("Ask three before me.")

Grading and Record Keeping

Now's a good time to revisit your ideas on the grading system and grade book; remember, you did that on page 54. Be sure that you know what the grading scale is in your district and at your grade level. Determine what types of assignments will count for a grade and how the grade will be figured, as with cooperative assignments. Also, think about how you will weigh assignments, projects, observations, tests, and homework. Teach the students your procedures for missing, incomplete, or late work.

What and How to Assess

Teachers need to validate student work by looking at it and giving feedback. I learned to limit the paper chase by not assigning classwork or homework that I didn't want to evaluate in some manner. Keep in mind that not every piece of work needs to be assessed the same way. Some assignments can be assessed quickly as you pick them up, while others require simple verbal feedback and still others need a more detailed examination.

On more extensive assignments, try focusing on only one trait. For example, if you have been teaching about character development and have your students write a story, assess it only for the depth and detail of character development, not for punctuation, content, handwriting, capital letters, use of interesting adjectives, and so on. You will get through the assignment faster by looking for one skill, *and* you and your students will be more likely to learn something from the assessment. Feedback on too many skills simultaneously rarely helps students improve.

Creating a Record-Keeping System

To keep track of student work, I create a portfolio for each student and start placing items in it right away. I maintained my *primary* students' portfolios in file folders. I chose to give *intermediate* students a three-ring binder (one batch of binders lasted me five years as I never let the binders leave school), divided into subject areas (reading, writing, spelling, math) and themes. Work was three-hole-punched and kept in the notebooks until the end of each grading period, when students chose a few pieces to place in the showcase portfolio; the rest went home.

Prepare a system for recording conferences, progress, and so forth. I used a four-inch binder to keep student information together. I arranged it alphabetically by first name and included a copy of the student information sheet, the printout from the school office, a conference sheet, assessments, copies of report cards, test printouts, and signed progress reports. When I needed to call parents, I just picked up the whole book and headed for the phone. You can also set up individual files; just make sure to refile them as soon as you make any additions to them so you can find them easily next time.

Timesaving Tip

For math and spelling assignments, have students write their answers down the page in the right-hand margin. Then place several papers side by side and scan across the pages, checking more than one paper at a time.

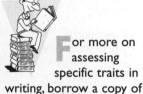

For more on assessing specific traits in writing, borrow a copy of *Seeing with New Eyes* by Vicki Spandel. It not only talks about assessing writing, but also about how to use what you learn from the assessments to better teach your students. It's a fantastic resource!

Homework

Make your homework reasonable and worthy of your students' time. Too much homework and students will be overwhelmed; too little and they won't be challenged. See the chart below for sample homework assignments.

A few years ago, a colleague shared her system for collecting her students' homework. As soon as the students came into the classroom in the morning, she had them place their homework on their desks and get started on their morning routines—read a book, figure out the daily math problem, write in their journal. She used this work time to visit with each student for a moment, ask if the homework was done and how he or she felt about it, and if there were any problems. She then *quickly* looked at the homework right there at the child's desk, noted its completion and correctness, stamped the work, and gave it back to the child. Students could then correct any errors, and the teacher was up to date on each child's performance. The key to the success of this technique is that students are meaningfully engaged during this brief time (10 to 20 minutes maximum) and they get immediate feedback on their work.

A final comment about homework: Remember that you will have a variety of levels of parent involvement each year. If possible, don't let homework become too large a part of your students' grades. Those students who have active parents will consistently turn in their homework done correctly. Those who don't may have little support with homework and may rarely complete the assignments. Penalizing students for their parents' inability to help at home just isn't fair. Find alternatives for students who need extra help—cross-age tutoring, working with the student first thing in the morning, giving the student an opportunity to start the homework in class. Do whatever it takes to help your students see homework as a positive, enriching experience.

Sample Homework

	Kindergarten	Primary/Intermediate
Sample Assignment	☼ Find object or picture that begins with the letter of the week. ☼ Sing a song about the letter of the week. ☼ Circle the letter of the week in texts.	☼ Read a book of choice. ☼ Practice spelling strategies. ☼ Practice math facts. ☼ Do background research on theme topics. ☼ Gather materials for in-class projects.
Suggested Length	☼ 5–10 minutes per night	☼ 30 minutes per night

Home and school are the biggest components of children's lives, so it's important for parents and teachers to have a productive relationship. This section presents ideas for introducing yourself to parents and maintaining communication with them throughout the year. In addition, parents can be a wonderful resource in the classroom; you'll find ideas for managing these motivated classroom helpers for the benefit of all.

Back-to-School Night

Many schools have a back-to-school night or open house early in the school year to give teachers a chance to meet the parents and establish a rapport with them as well as to share information about the classroom. See some ideas for a successful event at left.

One caution: You probably won't have time to address specific concerns that parents have about their children at this time, so it's important to let them know that you are interested in conferencing with them at another time. Beware the parent who monopolizes you with "So how's Jimmy doing in class?" It's your night to talk to the parents of *all* your students, not just one.

✦ Tip ✦

Ideas for a Successful Back-to-School Night

○ Have your students create invitations for their parents.

○ Display a variety of student work.

○ Make your curriculum available.

○ Set out any books that students will be using for the parents to peruse.

○ Prepare students to give their parents a tour of the room or even to do a scavenger hunt: "My favorite center is.... My best friend sits there.... When it's time to go home, I pick up my mail here...."

○ Have a sign-up sheet for parent helpers and another for parents who would like to talk to you in detail about their child's progress.

Keeping Parents Informed

During my first few years of teaching, I spent a great deal of time and effort creating a monthly newsletter to send home to parents. It was a daunting task, mainly because I considered myself lucky to know what was going to happen in my class one week in the future, not to mention a whole month to come! Then a colleague shared an article by Jane Baskwill entitled "Ask Me About—The Newsletter With a Difference" (*Teaching K–8*, May 1992). To inform parents of what was happening in the classroom, the author created a newsletter at the *end* of each week that included prompts so parents knew what kind of questions to ask their children about what they had learned. Instead of asking questions that are too general ("What did you do today?") or too broad ("What did you do in math?"), parents are clued into what has been happening in school during the week so they can encourage their children to talk in more detail about classroom learning experiences.

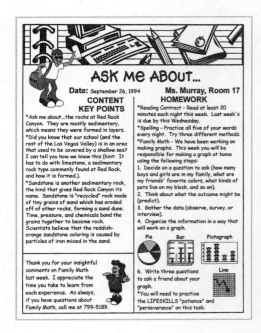

"Ask Me About" Newsletter

I adapted the "Ask Me About" newsletter to my classroom needs by first sitting down with my students each Friday and brainstorming all the things we had done during that week. Then I recorded their ideas in a notebook so I could easily transcribe them onto a sheet of ditto paper that evening. I chose the most important learnings that the students remembered and wrote them in the form of "Ask Me About" statements or questions. I found it worthwhile either to reduce the "Ask Me About" by half before copying it to send home, or put a progress report on the other half to save paper. On Monday afternoon, the students and I read through the completed and copied "Ask Me About" to jog their memories before taking it home. This step is important for review purposes as an entire weekend elapses between brainstorming and sending home the newsletter.

Examples of prompts I've used in newsletters include:

- **Ask me about...the writing process.** We are learning to go through six steps to write good stories. Do you know what they are?

- **Ask me about...research.** We are writing reports on volcanoes. I can tell you two reasons why plagiarism is wrong and show you how to use a Data Chart (see page 150) to keep from plagiarizing.

- **Ask me about...the rocks at Red Rock Canyon.** I can tell you two types of sedimentary rocks that can be found there. I can also sing a song about the rock cycle to help you understand.

- **Ask me about...telling time.** Help me practice telling time at home so I can do well on our Telling Time Bingo game on Wednesday.

- **Ask me about...Class Clown.** I can describe the main character and the setting to you.

"Ask Me About" Newsletter for K

With kindergartners, the "Ask Me About" had to be adapted. I used my computer to create a four-page booklet (the program Print Shop is easy and versatile!) to send home on Friday of each week. On the front, I listed information the parents needed to know about the upcoming week, such as homework, days off, and special events. I labeled the next page with a small circle, the next with a small square, and the last with a small triangle; these took the place of page numbers at the beginning of the year. At the top of the three pages were statements such as, "Ask me about the letter E. This week we learned a song about 'Elmo the Elephant' and the letter E. Ask me to sing the song for you two times." Then I left space where the children drew pictures to go along with the topic on each page. Sitting down together and practicing our drawing was fun and gave the children a visual cue when they went home to share the "Ask Me About" newsletter with their parents.

know you'll benefit by talking to your peers about back-to-school night or open house. Each school and district handles this important evening differently. Find out ahead of time what is expected of you.

Weekly Progress Reports

Weekly progress reports are another way of letting parents know how their children are doing in class, both academically and behaviorally. Progress reports range from the very specific, such as the Weekly Point Card (see page 183) or the Baseball Behavior Card (see page 184) to the very general (see pages 186–188). If you tell parents that progress reports will be coming home on a regular basis, be consistent about their distribution or students may face consequences at home for not bringing home their reports.

Telephone & Postcards

I also use the telephone to keep parents informed of individual challenges and successes—don't forget the successes! Rare is the parent who has heard from a teacher because his or her child did something great! You can also address several postcards to each parent at the first of the year, then periodically pull them out to send special notices or comments about student progress. It only takes a moment to write a note when the card has already been addressed and stamped. Just remember that it is necessary to maintain good records of what is said over the phone and in informal conferences (see page 188).

Parent Info Board

A wonderful hint from a colleague was to have a parent information board by the classroom door. Post information, schedules, questions, requests, and upcoming events on the board so parents can check to ensure that all student notices are making it home.

Remember that many of your students' parents may not have had positive experiences in school as children. Make them a part of your classroom program by involving them in their child's education every step of the way. Educate them on current issues through mini-workshops after school on topics such as the writing process, Family Math, or ways to help children at home. If you use few worksheets for teaching, parents may feel in the dark about how well their children are doing in school. I used to offer a standing invitation to parents to visit the classroom frequently and have their children share their portfolios with them. Let them know that you may be busy teaching or preparing for lessons, but that their children are capable of sharing what they have been doing in class. I have always been very fortunate in having supportive and considerate parents, but be cautious of parents who end up staying for extended amounts of time; you may find it necessary to schedule appointments with them to minimize disruptions to you and your students. Also, be aware that many schools require parents to check in at the office to receive a visitor's badge prior to visiting the classroom. Remind parents to follow the appropriate procedure.

Involving Parents as Classroom Helpers

Using parents as helpers is another way to involve them in their child's education. They can be a great asset to your classroom if they understand the nature of the jobs you want them to do and respect your need to teach instead of chat with them. Talk to other teachers at your site to find out what works for them, as the characteristics of each parent population varies. Parents can:

- organize class parties
- assist with field trips
- work with individual students
- create classroom materials
- locate classroom resources
- organize class fundraisers
- make copies
- prepare materials for lessons

Some parents will even volunteer to do some work at home if their schedules conflict with school hours.

If parents will be assisting you with complex tasks such as working with students on publishing books, you will need to train them well. Consider having a short workshop after school to prepare them for their new "job." For example, at the beginning of the year, I asked parents for assistance in these three areas: parties, field trips, and student publishing. In October, I trained those parents who had expressed an interest in helping with student publishing so they would have adequate knowledge of the writing process and conferencing when the students were ready to publish. The other parents took care of organizing field trips and class parties, two tasks that can be very time-consuming for a new teacher.

It is essential that parent helpers actually *help*, rather than chat with you. Whatever system you decide to use, try to have materials for parent helpers in a regular location and let parents know what they'll be doing ahead of time. Parents will be able to get right to work without disturbing your teaching time.

As you are working through the first few weeks of school, you should review any standards for teachers that your district or state might have. This will help you stay on the right track and prepare you for your first evaluation as a teacher. Reread your vision and add two more items to your action plan so you can continue monitoring your growth and progress.

Taking care of yourself at this time is crucial to being able to persist through the downhill slide of the new-teacher cycle. Devote one day to catching up on your sleep, take vitamin C, eat healthy foods, wash your hands frequently, and do something FUN! Get out of your classroom and connect with other teachers real-time or online to network and share ideas, frustrations, and joys.

The First Year of Teaching

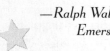

old on a minute! Before we work on anything else, we need to take a little side trip. Parent-teacher conferences typically occur in the fall, so let's get ready for them now.

Now that you've made it through the first month, you're ready to hone your teaching skills and learn new teaching techniques. Because each state, district, and even school has its own way of doing things, matters of curriculum and how to teach the various subjects are beyond the scope of this book. In this section you will find ideas for instruction related to the fundamental skills of teaching. Check your school for specific applications of the ideas presented in this section.

Parent-Teacher Conferences

When the time comes for your first round of parent-teacher conferences, don't worry; the parents and students will probably be more anxious than you are! At the mere mention of a conference, many parents flash back to the conferences *their* parents attended, and the results of those visits. It can be a completely frightening situation for parents. Below are some hints I received as a second-year teacher that helped smooth the way for successful parent-teacher conferences.

Plan

☼ **Gather parent information.** Several weeks prior to conference time, schools may send a letter to parents listing times and dates of parent conferences and including a section where parents can request a time for their child's conference. Getting information returned to you can take a while, and some parents may not respond, so leave yourself plenty of time to collect the information you will need in order to set up a schedule.

☼ **Check with the teachers of your students' siblings.** Coordinating schedules for parent convenience will be greatly appreciated!

☼ **Create a schedule.** The expected length of conferences varies from school to school. I try to leave myself a breather every four to five conferences, scheduling conferences that I suspect may be stressful next to conferences which will most likely be "easy."

☼ **Send home one or more reminders.** Be sure to allow parents adequate time to arrange their schedules to meet with you (many schools already have forms developed for this purpose).

☼ **Let parents know if you expect their child to attend the conference.** I truly enjoyed having students join their parents at conferences. Several years ago at conference time, I had the opportunity to show a parent how to play with her child; she just didn't know what to do with her very active kindergartner at home.

☼ **Prepare the final schedule.** Write up the finalized schedule to post outside of your door for parent reference, and make a copy to keep with you in the room.

☼ **Arrange for a translator if necessary.** Do this as far in advance as possible—your librarian, custodian, school nurse, school aide, or principal will be vigorously recruited by teachers for translation services if they are fluent in another language!

Having children present at parent-teacher conferences will give you a chance to model how to talk to a child, and it is a visual reminder that the child (rather than the parent) is the focus of the conference.

Prepare

☼ **Have materials handy.** Set aside materials that parents may need in order to have a productive and organized conference, such as note paper, pencils, school evaluations, and other information you plan to pass out. Each grading period, I made a copy of all report cards. The copies were great for making notes on and were lifesavers if the real report card got misplaced. Place the report cards and copies, student files, work samples, portfolios, test results, and so on in folders for each child, then stack them in the order of your conference schedule. I also have a checklist of additional information I intend to share at each conference, such as information on class programs, field trips, and homework.

☼ **Be ready to take notes.** Ask the school office if official conference forms are available for recording what is discussed and the actions that need to be taken by the parent, teacher, and student. If not, you may want to keep a class list handy to make notes dealing with follow-ups and things you must remember to do after the conferences are over. Forgetting things that need to be followed up on is easy, especially when dealing with several conferences each day.

☼ **Check parents' names.** Find out your parents' names. Calling a parent by her child's last name only to find out that he or she has a different last name can be embarassing.

☼ **Create a comfortable environment.** Arrange the conference environment so parents can be comfortable. If you are teaching in the primary grades, remember that first-grade chairs are difficult for anyone but first graders to sit on! Keep the setting informal by avoiding physical barriers. If you choose to sit behind your desk, you appear to place yourself in opposition to the parents. I preferred to hold conferences at a table, where I could sit beside the parent. This kind of a setup was warmer and less threatening for both of us.

☼ **Keep the time in mind.** Place your seat where you can easily glance at a clock. Some teachers set a timer as each conference begins.

The Conference

☼ **Greet parents.** Welcome parents at the door in a positive, confident manner. You have been trained for this job and are well qualified to address your students' progress. Be friendly and put the parents at ease, but remember that they're here to discuss their child.

☼ **Conduct the conference.** Walk through the report card and share your questions and concerns before opening up the floor to parents. Show examples of student work. No matter how you structure the conference, be honest, firm, and positive about each student. Refrain from using educational jargon, such as IEP, ESL, or GATE. If we want to enlist parents as partners, making them feel inadequate or uneducated only dampens their desire to be involved in their child's education. It is sometimes tempting to suggest that parents get extra help for their child; however, recommending tutors, learning clinics, counseling, and other services may cause the school or school district to become responsible for program costs.

☼ **Plan follow-up.** Each conference should end with a moment to plan for follow-up or interventions. Both you and the parents should be clear about the goals. Remind parents to sign and return the report cards, if necessary, and invite them to visit with any specialists who are available. Be aware that student records are legally available to parents. If parents wish to see their child's records, refer them to your administrator.

☼ **Dealing with challenging situations.** You may have the challenge of dealing with a difficult situation during a conference. Be strong enough to know when you have reached your limits. If you expect that the conference will be difficult based on past encounters with the parent in question, consider requesting that your administrator or a specialist be present. If the conference unexpectedly takes a negative turn, perhaps you could tell the parent that you would like to spend more time than you have available to discuss the situation, then reschedule the conference at a time when the principal can join you. Do not force yourself to stay in a potentially dangerous situation. Extricate yourself as gracefully and professionally as possible.

If you weren't nervous before, you probably are now! Still, it's important to be prepared for whatever may come, and you'll be pleasantly surprised in most cases.

I suggest that you sit down with another teacher for a role-playing session. Think of situations that might come up at parent-teacher conferences and practice how you might handle them. It may feel strange, but it's infinitely better to try it out now rather than wait until the real thing.

Managing Your Time

One of the most important resources a teacher has is time. In a busy school day, there never seems to be enough of it. Because so little of a student's year is spent in the classroom, teachers must continually seek ways to save time spent on non-instructional activities and maximize the effectiveness of time spent with students.

Stephen Covey, noted author on the subject of working effectively and efficiently, describes four types of activities on which we spend our time:

☼ **Urgent and important**—Crises; pressing problems; deadline-driven projects, meetings, and preparations. *Example: A parent standing at your door, demanding to talk to you about her child's progress.*

☼ **Important but not urgent**—Preparation; prevention; values clarification; planning; relationship-building; true re-creation; empowerment. *Example: Searching the library and your files, and asking a colleague for resources to plan a unit on the rain forest, which you will be starting in a month.*

☼ **Urgent but not important**—Interruptions; some phone calls, mail, reports, and meetings; many proximate, pressing matters; many popular activities. *Example: Creating a graphic organizer for your lesson tomorrow. You could create a handwritten one, but you'd prefer to do it on the computer so you can add graphics and fancy fonts before copying it for your class.*

☼ **Neither important nor urgent**—Trivia; busywork; junk mail; time-wasters; "escape" activities; those activities we do so we can procrastinate an important task. *Example: Rearranging classroom furniture, even though the current arrangement is working well and has only been in place for a couple of weeks.*

Covey believes that if we can better manage the unimportant activities in our lives, we will have more time for those "important but not urgent" things that are essential, such as "re-creating" ourselves through recreation and "sharpening the saw" of our professional lives.

As teachers, we perform countless non-instructional tasks to prepare for the precious time we have with our students. We plan lessons, prepare materials, decorate the classroom, grade papers, read about professional issues, participate in staff meetings, take classes, refer students for special services, and much more. The trick is in balancing preparatory activities so we are well prepared but also have enough energy to teach what we have prepared. As a new teacher, it was frustrating to spend hours getting ready for my lessons, then being too tired to teach them well. Let's discuss some areas in which you can save time (and free up energy) for actual teaching.

Check out Susan and Steven Mamchak's *Teacher's Time Management Survival Kit* for some time-saving techniques and materials.

If you've not yet read Stephen Covey's work, you might want to treat yourself to a little professional reading in *First Things First*, where Covey goes into great detail on time-management techniques.

Rooting Out Procrastination and Perfectionism

Ross Van Ness of Ball State University says that when we procrastinate, unpleasant tasks become more unpleasant, making the task and the discomfort associated with performing it even more difficult to deal with later. He suggests that procrastinators follow these three steps:

☼ break tasks into smaller parts
("success by the yard is hard; by the inch, it's a cinch")

☼ do the unpleasant task first thing in the morning
("eat a live toad for breakfast and the rest of the day will be a breeze")

☼ deal with one unpleasantry before tackling another
("chase one rabbit at a time")

Sometimes a task just needs to be seen in a different light by talking about it to someone, working on it backwards, or brainstorming every solution, workable or not. Procrastination puts the task in charge of you, rather than you in charge of the task.

Those "neither important nor urgent" activities are often rooted in perfectionism. Rather than work on something important, such as grading, I sometimes choose unimportant tasks, such as perfecting the organization of my classroom library in order to put off the big task. If you have a penchant for perfection, try to get beyond it in the classroom or you will waste hours of precious time "getting it right." Choose to spend your precious time "perfecting" those things that really matter—for example, proofreading parent letters to make sure they reflect professional work.

Maintaining Your Professional Network

Spend a moderate amount of time in the lounge engaging in professional dialogue. There is so much to be learned from other teachers; use every opportunity to find out what they do that is successful. Consider maintaining a network of teachers from other schools, too; e-mail and the Internet can keep you in touch with people all over the country.

Although talking with others can help you maintain perspective, be aware of negative people. They waste your time and drain the precious energy you need to be an effective teacher. Politely let them know that you are not interested in gossip and that you have many things to do to prepare for your students; then remove yourself from the situation with a minimum of fuss. The students need you to be at your best every minute you're at school. Don't let your students down by letting someone else bring you down!

Streamlining Classroom Activity

Agenda

Keep an agenda of the day's activities on the board so your students won't have to ask you all day long, "What are we going to do next?" Initially, I attached times to my agenda; however, I found that my students were overly concerned about staying on that schedule. They would tell me, "It's time to start math" just when I'd decided to extend writing. I experimented with several types of agendas and found this to be the most successful: I made some agenda pieces labeled with daily activities, laminated them, and put magnet strips on the back of them so they would attach easily to my board. Then I could just slide them into place each day and move them if necessary (see pages 177–180). I eventually got help with that job, too. A student helper would look at my lesson plans and take a few minutes when school started each day to put up the agenda so I could begin teaching.

Once these agenda pieces were made, it took very little time and effort to change my agenda each day.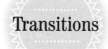

Transitions

Go back and review your classroom procedures and routines (see pages 49–53). Any activity that can become automatic for your students is going to save time and frustration. Solid procedures can help you minimize the time that transitions take. Keeping transitions short and focused prevents many problems that can eat up your time and cause unnecessary conflicts in the classroom. To keep kids on track during transitions:

☼ have students model your class rules and procedures

☼ time students on their transitions and challenge them to beat their previous record

☼ wind up a music box at the beginning of the day, open it before transitions and close it when students are ready; if music is left at the end of the day, they have "won"

When transitions are taking longer than you wish, review the procedures with the children and practice, practice, practice!

Routines

Squeezing a huge curriculum into a short time period is always a challenge. To make every minute count, create routines to maximize the time that you do have. One of my favorite routines in grades two through four happened first thing in the morning. My students began silent reading immediately while I took care of the lunch count, attendance, parent inquiries, and assisted students who needed extra help. After 15 minutes, they completed a short daily writing assignment on the reading: a letter to me, a summary, a prediction, a description of the main character or setting, or a response to the author's style. Within the first 25 minutes of each day, the students practiced reading, generated a piece of writing, showed me how well they comprehended what they read, and started the day off in a relaxed but engaged manner.

Planning Effective Practice

Another time-saving principle is "less is more." We know that concept building *and* skill practice are both important in all areas of the curriculum. But do students really need to do 30 problems to prove that they understand? Consider the child who does them all wrong; he has practiced the skill incorrectly 30 times and now must go back to the beginning to undo the damage! Teach a concept, then provide opportunities for guided and independent practice, but on a limited scale. If a student can do 10 problems correctly, then he has proven his facility with the content. Skill practice on a grander scale can occur at home or during free time at school.

One quick and popular way to practice a number of skills on a daily basis is math calendar ("Every Day Counts," "Math Their Way," "Opening Eyes to Mathematics," and so on) or Mountain Math where students practice math skills every day by working through one or two problems as a class. In my third-grade class, we patterned, added, subtracted, skip counted, multiplied, divided, weighed, measured, graphed, and estimated every day to keep those skills and concepts fresh and in use. This helped my students retain information better than when I taught subtraction for a month, then left it to teach other skills until review time at the end of the year.

Planning for Integrated Instruction

Integrated instruction is a method for organizing instruction to *synthesize* more than one subject area, rather than *separating* instruction by subject area. The first year I did any full-time integrated instruction, my school went on double sessions from August to early March so we could share our campus with a new school not yet completed. I remember looking at my long-range plan for the year, wondering how I was going to teach everything that was required in a much shorter day. The answer was integration. I realized that if I taught science during reading, social studies during writing, or health during math, I just might be able to get through all the curriculum by the end of the year.

The results were so exciting that I continued to integrate the subject areas even when my school stopped double sessions. I found that I enjoyed teaching language and math through the filters of science, social studies, and health more than separating the disciplines. I noticed, too, that my students were highly motivated and, in general, seemed to be able to remember their lessons more readily. The students had a deeper understanding of the content and started making connections between the subject areas that, up until that time, I didn't believe elementary children could make.

Integrated instruction has many faces. A *unit* is a grouping of activities based on a common *topic*, such as weather or pets. A *theme* is a grouping of activities based on a common *concept*, such as change or exploration. If your goal for integrating instruction is to deepen student understanding, help students make connections between disciplines, and connect learning to real life, then you will want to create themes based on concepts.

Planning for Integration

I enjoyed designing integrated instruction with a partner. The ideas flowed freely, and the end product was much more instructionally solid than when I planned alone. Below, I've listed the thought process I used for my beginning themes. Grab a partner and a pizza and get started!

1. Which science, social studies, or health topics are of interest to my students and to me?
2. Which of those topics can be related to my state or district curriculum?
3. What is the big idea (concept) behind the topic I want to integrate?
4. What do I know about the topic I want to integrate?
5. What do the students already know or think they know about the topic?
6. What do I want the students to know and understand about the topic?
7. What do I want the students to be able to do by the end of the theme?
8. What resources are available for teaching about the topic?

❝ *A*sk yourself... How am I changing a child's life with what I teach today? **❞**

Susan Kovalik and Karen Olsen authored *Exceeding Expectations: A User's Guide to Implementing Brain Research in the Classroom.* This groundbreaking book assists the reader in developing a yearlong concept-based theme. This is not exactly a baby step! I only mention it because once you become more comfortable with the day-to-day operations of a classroom, this model will strengthen your instruction. Toward the end of this year or maybe this summer, locate the book and flex your teaching muscles!

9. Which skills can be drawn out of the available materials and which skills require additional resources?

10. What activities and experiences are appropriate for teaching the skills and exploring the concept?

11. In what order will I present the content and activities?

12. How will I help the students collect and organize their work?

13. How will I assess the students' work?

14. How will I culminate the unit?

Integrated Days

If integrated instruction is new to you, you may want to start by developing an integrated day—one day that employs several subject areas to develop a single topic. When I first began teaching, I developed one-day content themes based around holidays. For these special days, I set aside my regular plans and substituted integrated activities. On Columbus Day, my first graders:

- listened to the story of Columbus

- estimated then measured the size of his ships

- built a model of the ships

- wrote a short story about sailing with Columbus

- tried out a surveyor's tools

- built a class compass with a needle, a piece of Styrofoam, and a container of water

- played Weathervane, a game in which students practice jumping around in place to face each of the cardinal directions

If you would like to "test the waters" by creating an integrated day, choose your topic. Once you have determined the day(s) you plan to integrate, search through your curriculum for objectives that can become a part of your day. Conscientiously teach those skills through the topic and remember to review and reinforce them in other contexts throughout the year to ensure retention and understanding.

Literature Unit

You may also choose to develop an integrated unit around a piece of literature. A literature theme can be united by a concept, too, if you are ready for that step. When trade books first arrived on the school scene, I began to experiment with using a book as the basis of a theme. One of the first literature themes I created was based upon *Cloudy with a Chance of Meatballs* by Judi Barrett. I read the book and was immediately charmed by

Things to Think About

Halloween Integrated Day

- read books about spiders

- observe several types of spiders on loan from a pet store

- diagram the parts of a spider

- draw an imaginary spider and describe it in writing

- do a spider search on the playground

- make spider cookies out of Oreos and black licorice

- compare the number of legs on a spider with legs on a person, dog, chair, bird, or ant

- watch a filmstrip about spiders

its humorous and fanciful content. Once I had decided that it was meaty enough to make into a unit, I created the planning web below.

After developing that first literature theme, I discovered Perfection Learning Company's Beyond the Basal series of teacher's guides and Scholastic Inc.'s Innovations, each devoted to a noted piece of children's literature. These guides helped me develop literature themes more quickly and got me thinking about how I could make the themes more expansive, especially where skills were concerned.

Once I started brainstorming ideas for this literature theme, I couldn't stop!

▼

Reading

◆ Fact and fantasy
◆ Alphabetical order (alphabetize foods)
◆ Alliteration
◆ Cause and effect
◆ Imagery
◆ Comparatives and superlatives
◆ Vowel dipthongs [ou/ow (cloud), oi/oy (joy), ew (blew)]

Literature

◆ *The Cloud Book*
◆ *Questions and Answers About Weather*
◆ *Weather Words and What They Mean*
◆ *Storms*
◆ *Could Be Worse*
◆ *Grandpa's Too-Good Garden*
◆ *Song and Dance Man*
◆ *Blackberries in the Dark*
◆ *The War with Grandpa*
◆ *What Happens to a Hamburger?*
◆ *Roxaboxen*
◆ *My Little Island*

Math

◆ Graphing (favorite foods, trends)
◆ Reading a thermometer
◆ Adding calories from food cards to determine an appropriate meal
◆ Subtracting food prices in newspaper ads from $10 to get as close to $0 as possible
◆ Making change at class "grocery" store
◆ Geometry of food objects
◆ Symmetry of food objects
◆ Spaghetti and meatball storyboards

Cloudy with a Chance of Meatballs

Science, Health, Social Studies

◆ Weather
◆ Mapping an imaginary land
◆ Families (Adopt-a-Grandparent)
◆ Communities
◆ Nutrition
◆ Properties (sink or float)

Language

◆ Tall tales
◆ Newspaper articles (writing a story for the *Chew and Swallow*)
◆ Innovating on a book like *On Market Street*

Art, Music, P. E.

◆ Building stacked sandwiches
◆ Learning a tap dance ("Song and Dance Man")
◆ Building a model of a town
◆ Preparing a concert for a senior citizens' home

Extended Theme

As you become more comfortable with integration, you may create a theme that will last a month or so. At this point, the theme must be grounded in a concept. Month-long themes based on a topic rather than a concept and rationale can become tiresome for students and teachers, and often fail to result in deep understanding of anything meaningful, as they may focus on learning facts related to the topic rather than creating connections to be carried over into life.

Assessing the Theme

When I began doing extended themes, organization of student papers and projects became an issue. I had each student create a folder out of a 12- by 18-inch sheet of white construction paper to decorate according to the theme. Students placed all assignments related to the theme inside the folder to keep them organized and neat. At the end of the theme, we went through the folders as a class and put all the papers in order. Each student listed the assignments; graded himself or herself on a plus, check, or minus scale; then wrote a comment about why he or she earned that grade.

I used the theme folders to assess both content knowledge and skill development. For example, a piece of writing about recycling could be used to evaluate nonfiction reading skills, informative writing skills, and knowledge about recycling. Theme folders can be shared with parents, displayed on a bulletin board, or added to student portfolios. Ask your librarian to see if he or she would let your students display their finished theme folders and projects in the library; many libraries even have display cases for that purpose.

The multiple intelligences (see page 134–135) are very useful tools for assessing themes. We sometimes forget that students can demonstrate the understanding of concepts and the facility with skills through several mediums. The written test has its place in education, but don't let it become your sole method for finding out if your students are achieving the lesson goals. Students who understand content can demonstrate their understanding by writing or speaking about it (verbal-linguistic), analyzing it (logical-mathematical), acting it out (bodily-kinesthetic), drawing it (visual-spatial), chanting it (musical-rhythmic), or tying it to nature (environmental-naturalist). Some assessments should be teacher's choice and others should be student's choice to ensure a balance.

Assess for thinking skills, which should be enhanced if the theme is an effective one. Watch students for evidence that they can predict, categorize, or infer at the beginning of the theme. Check for observation skills, reporting, or classifying during theme activities. As the theme progresses, there should be signs of students sequencing, summarizing, justifying, and applying the content of the theme.

Determine which information you need to evaluate student performance and the effectiveness of the theme. I emphasized effort and initiative in grading themes. Please remember that every district has its own philosophy of grading and will have certain expectations. Find out what other teachers at your school are doing to assess themes so you can conform to school standards.

Help students learn organizational skills by creating and maintaining theme folders.

Instruction

Multiple Intelligences

In the early 1980s, Howard Gardner's theory of multiple intelligences took the educational world by storm. Educators had long dabbled in learning modalities—verbal, auditory, tactile, and kinesthetic methods for receiving information—and recognized that all students do not learn the same way. The multiple intelligences go beyond learning modalities, as they deal with the way information is processed and how learning occurs in individuals. In his research, Gardner identified a minimum of eight "intelligences," problem-solving and product-producing capabilities.

Stop reading and take a minute to grab a friend and explain how to parallel park. Chances are, you used several of the multiple intelligences to solve this problem!

- ☼ verbal-linguistic
- ☼ logical-mathematical
- ☼ visual-spatial
- ☼ bodily-kinesthetic
- ☼ musical-rhythmic
- ☼ intrapersonal
- ☼ interpersonal
- ☼ environmental-naturalist

Recently, Gardner added a ninth intelligence (existentialist) to the list. Because the ninth intelligence is so new, not much has been written about it yet, particularly about its applications in the classroom, if any. Keep your eyes and ears open for new information!

Many books and articles sprang from Gardner's work, some of which are truer to the theory than others. As you look at resources devoted to the multiple intelligences, make sure that they are not just collections of "fun" activities. If the activities don't focus on solving problems or producing products, they probably aren't valid applications of the theory.

As you look at each intelligence, think about how you could apply it to your classroom instruction. Keep in mind that the intelligences are manifested in different ways; for example, a verbal-linguistic child who has complementary interpersonal strengths may be a talker, whereas a verbal-linguistic child who is more intrapersonal may be a writer.

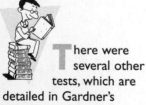

There were several other tests, which are detailed in Gardner's first book about the intelligences—*Frames of Mind*. Reading the book is not a walk in the park, but if you want to understand the original thinking behind the theory, that's the place to go. Gardner recently clarified and extended his theory in *Intelligence Reframed*.

☼ **verbal-linguistic** (word strong)—These students speak, read, or write well. They like manipulating words (jokes and puns) and playing with language (word games). To develop verbal-linguistic intelligence, have students read and write in a variety of genres, give speeches, participate in performances, and hear the magic of language by reading and telling stories. Have them create word games, crossword puzzles, and word searches. Model *your* love of language.

☼ **logical-mathematical** (math strong)—These students are good with numbers and enjoy logic problems and puzzles. They enjoy figuring things out and coming up with unusual solutions. To develop logical-mathematical intelligence, use Think Alouds for solving mathematical problems. Ask students how they came up with the answer, why they think it's right, and if they can think of another way to solve the problem. Have them record information on graphs, establish time lines, and create maps. Let them explore how things work.

☼ **visual-spatial** (space strong)—These students doodle and design. They "see" things differently in their minds, and they recognize spatial relationships. To develop visual-spatial intelligence, read stories with well-described visual images, such as *James and the Giant Peach*. Have students listen to the words the author uses and draw a picture from the description. Say, "I feel like I'm really there because I can 'see' what's happening." Let students demonstrate understanding through drawing, painting, sculpting, and creating backdrops and scenery for class plays. Use videos, slides, art, puzzles, and mazes.

☼ **bodily-kinesthetic** (body strong)—These students are capable of coordinated and expressive fine- or large-motor activities. They are good at sports, dance, tying their shoes (and untying knots in other people's shoes!), and other physical activities. To build bodily-kinesthetic intelligence, give students opportunities to role play, act out stories, participate in physical simulations of concepts (e.g., act out the processes of the heart by role playing the blood cells), build models, and move to music. Movement is typically a great need for children who are bodily-kinesthetic. Don't insist that they sit still at their desks with both feet flat on the floor; their learning is enhanced if they are allowed to move.

☼ **musical-rhythmic** (music strong)—These students are affected by music, rhythm, and environmental sounds. They sing, whistle, hum, tap, and sway. They are able to attach feelings to music and can create and replicate tunes. To build musical-rhythmic intelligence, have students create songs or raps to explain concepts (e.g., a song describing the rock cycle), put their own learning to music, or participate in music and dance from a variety of sources. Play different types of music during the day.

☼ **environmental-naturalist** (nature strong)—These students have empathy for stranded crickets and butterflies with broken wings. They seem to "come alive" when allowed to interact with nature. They are able to see patterns and relationships in nature and life. To develop environmental intelligence, read stories about environmental issues to your students, categorize and classify objects of all kinds, or turn your classroom into a nature lab complete with plants and animals. Conduct lessons outside on occasion or even create a playground nature area as a school service project—"nature-strong" students will be happy to maintain it!

☼ **interpersonal** (people strong)—These students are sensitive to other people's needs and moods. They excel at cooperative activities and solving conflicts between classmates. To develop interpersonal intelligence, use cooperative learning, have students tutor each other, and

All children, especially logical thinkers, enjoy discovering how things work. And the book, *How Things Work*, by David Macauley, is great for the logical-mathematical mind.

found an interesting survey for the multiple intelligences at **www.surfaquarium.com /MIinvent.htm**. The Web is loaded with MI information!

Succeeding with Multiple Intelligences: Teaching Through the Personal Intelligences from The New City School (1-314-361-6411) is a comprehensive resource. Skylight Publishing and The Brain Store offer a multitude of MI resources.

teach students methods for solving group problems, perhaps using class meetings as a forum for social problem solving. Let them interact with others when problem solving. Don't insist that they quietly work alone much of the time; they need to talk to be productive. Instead, teach them procedures for using a "one-inch voice" (a voice that doesn't go further than "one inch" from their lips).

intrapersonal (self strong)—These students are self-motivated and reflective. They watch and listen, taking in conversation rather than contributing to it. They prefer working alone, need quiet time to process new ideas, and daydream often. They often need space and time away from the hustle and bustle of the classroom agenda so they can pursue ideas in their own way. To develop intrapersonal intelligence, give students time at the end of each day to reflect on what they have learned and experienced in a journal, involve them in setting personal goals, and allow them to work at their own pace. Share your own reflections, listing two or three reasons why the day was a good one.

Planning With Intelligence

The Variation Approach

When first beginning instruction using strategies compatible with the multiple intelligences, students will need to participate in a wide variety of experiences to learn about their preferences. The teacher's lessons rotate among the intelligences. All students complete the activities.

The Choice Approach

If the students are widely varied in their preferred intelligence or unsure of their preferences, the teacher offers a choice in each intelligence to the students. Students complete one or more activities.

The Bridge Approach

If the intelligence demand is primarily in one intelligence, the activity is focused on that intelligence. All students do the activity together, and the teacher offers bridging techniques to help students deal with the intelligence and the content in a successful manner.

Keep in mind that the multiple intelligences are *problem-solving capabilities*. Allow students to use all the intelligences to solve a problem—read about it, analyze it, draw it, act it out, work to a rhythm, relate it to nature, talk about it, or reflect on it. Having multiple ways to solve a problem is beneficial for all of us, particularly when problems are complex and require innovative thinking.

Multitudes of educational applications have been developed based on multiple intelligence theory. I use the intelligences in planning and instruction by providing a balance of experiences in each of the intelligences. I've provided examples of three teaching structures (left) that can be used to address the intelligences in your classroom. I typically implement the structures sequentially, using the variation approach at the beginning of the year, then adding student choices, and finally, teaching bridging techniques to the students. A combination of these structures ensures a balance of activities to meet the needs of all your students. The multiple intelligences also make great assessments.

Learning Centers

Learning centers are one way to involve students in learning. They can provide reinforcement of newly learned skills as well as opportunities for children to discover new ideas for themselves. They allow children to interact with other students and to manipulate learning materials. I'll offer a few ideas to help you get started with centers in your classroom, but you'll want to explore the many books that have been written on the subject.

Successful learning centers exhibit several characteristics. They:

- ☼ are tied to the curriculum
- ☼ reinforce skills
- ☼ help students discover concepts
- ☼ have a built-in system for accountability
- ☼ include a variety of activities, not just paper and pencil tasks
- ☼ are carefully taught
- ☼ have clear directions so students are able to work independently
- ☼ allow for student choice

This last characteristic is worthy of pages of discussion, but I'll keep it simple. A strict rotation of centers doesn't give children the opportunity to practice self-direction and responsibility as a learner. Rotations can simplify the organization of the students, but choice helps them learn more than just the content of the centers.

Keep in mind that choice doesn't mean a free-for-all. In kindergarten, children can visit a variety of centers or choose activities from a central area and then put them back when they are finished, free to choose another. In first and second grade, each center may have a limited number of spaces. As the spaces are filled, students need to select a different center. To make this concept concrete for young students, put labeled clothespins or necklaces at each center. As a child selects the center, he or she takes a clothespin or necklace. When the labels for a center are gone, students know to select another center. In third and fourth grade, centers may take on a different look. They might be independent or small-group "explorations" that are laid out in the room or placed in file folders for students to select. Some of my favorite intermediate explorations were drawn from the multiple intelligences:

- ☼ write a script about…
- ☼ create a diagram of…
- ☼ make a model of…
- ☼ compare and contrast with a Venn diagram…
- ☼ journal your observations of…
- ☼ create a song about…
- ☼ create a cartoon to show the sequence of…

Some of my favorite books on managing learning centers are Linda Holliman's *The Complete Guide to Classroom Centers, The Complete Learning Center Book* (this book integrates curriculum in each center and even includes vocabulary that could be taught in conjunction with each center), and those from Creative Teaching Press.

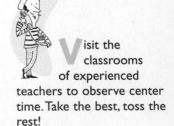
Visit the classrooms of experienced teachers to observe center time. Take the best, toss the rest!

Whatever shape your centers take, you will want to make sure that students know what to do at each center as well as how to behave. One kindergarten teacher that I visited had a book of photographs that showed students how to use each center. She shared the book each morning before children went one by one to choose their favorite. This teacher also offered controlled choices by designating some centers as have-to's and others as can-do's. During the center period, students were required to do some activities and could choose others. Last but not least, have a signal for getting students' attention and a procedure for cleaning up and moving to the next activity.

Incorporate a variety of skills into your centers. This student is "calling the vet" to make an appointment for her sick (stuffed) kitten.

Grouping

Students learn in different ways, so teachers need to provide a variety of grouping structures to strike a balance between interpersonal and intrapersonal activities. The classroom where children only work in groups doesn't allow students to build an individual work ethic. The classroom where children don't have an opportunity to collaborate doesn't prepare students for the "real" world. Structure daily activities for pairs, trios, small groups, and the whole group. The keys to success with grouping include having students collaborate only when the project requires collaboration, being actively involved when students work in groups, varying groups according to student needs, and teaching students how to work successfully in groups.

To create random groups, try Jungle Jabber (adapted from *Tribes* by Jeanne Gibbs). Create pictures of different jungle animals. You'll need one type of animal for each group you wish to form. Duplicate, cut, and fold in half enough animal squares for your class. Place the folded pictures in a basket for students to select. When you give a signal, students must find their new groups by making the sound that the animal makes—they may not talk or show their pictures, only make their animal's sound. You can also create random groupings by cutting one piece of construction paper into two to four puzzle pieces for each group, depending on the number of students you want to have in each group. Distribute the pieces randomly and have students work together to find out where their puzzle pieces belong. When they complete their "people puzzle," they'll know who is in their group for that particular task.

Below are some ideas (adapted from *The Reading Teacher*, Vol. 44, No. 8, April 1991, page 538) for using various grouping structures in your classroom. As you plan a lesson, consider which type(s) of grouping best fits your needs.

Whole Group...

Working as a whole group creates and maintains the class culture, promotes the feeling of the class as a learning community, provides a forum for transmission of information needed by all students, and allows for whole group brainstorming. *Use a whole-group structure for introduction to common skills and concepts, cooperative decision making, solving class problems, choral reading, teacher or student demonstrations, shared experiences, performances, and celebrations.*

Small Group...

- TRIBE—a social group that remains together for the entire school year. *Use for developing small "families" within the classroom to which students can turn for companionship, comfort, problem solving, assistance with any number of issues, and individual celebrations.*

- LEARNING CLUB—a flexible group whose membership varies based on common interests; may change daily, weekly, or as projects are completed. *Use interest-based learning clubs for research topics, content-area explorations, and enrichment.*

- FLEXIBLE-NEEDS GROUP—a group whose membership changes when the skill has been mastered. *Use flexible needs groups for remediation when your assessments show you that clarification of skills and concepts is necessary. Use as enrichment for students who have already mastered the skill currently being learned by the rest of the class.*

- MIXED-ABILITY GROUP—a group whose members exhibit a wide variety of achievement levels in all areas of the curriculum, social skills, and the multiple intelligences. *Use for academic support groups (tutoring), such as reading, writing, and math, as well as student-created projects and productions (writing and producing plays, creating songs, building models, creating artwork, designing dances).*

Pairs...

Working in pairs gives students more opportunities to be actively involved in social and academic situations. Pairs may be self-selected or teacher-assigned. *Use for research, free-choice reading, math practice, peer or cross-age tutoring, writing conferences, problem solving, sharing, and art projects.*

Individuals...

Working alone allows for uninterrupted reading, writing, mathematics, and research; personal choice; personal reflection; personal pacing; and individual achievement. *Use for sustained reading and writing, personal investigation, journal writing, choosing resources, reflection, self-evaluation, goal setting, and skill and concept assessment.*

HARMONY
調
The way of working together

聽
Listen

會心
Communicate

意守
Concentrate

激賞
Appreciate

自制
Control Yourself

讓
Yield

▲

"Harmony" when working together is defined for students on this wall display.

Read anything related to cooperative learning by Johnson and Johnson and Kagan. Two other great resources I have found on creating a cooperative classroom are *Tribes* by Jeanne Gibbs and *Cooperative Learning: Where Heart Meets Mind* by Bennett, Rolheiser-Bennett, and Stevahn. Both books detail research related to cooperative learning, current trends in education, and preparing students for life through collaboration.

Cooperative Learning

Teachers who use a variety of grouping structures in their classrooms find it necessary to teach their students how to cooperate. Jeanne Gibbs (*Tribes*) created excellent guidelines for cooperative learning, which I used for several years in my primary classroom (attentive listening, appreciation, no put-downs, right to pass, and mutual respect). Then I developed my own, "Harmony" (adapted from ancient Japanese principles of the samurai), to go with a theme unit on Asia.

According to Johnson and Johnson, students need to understand the importance of working together. They identify five basic elements that help students work effectively in small groups:

☼ **Positive Interdependence**—Students must feel connected to each other in the accomplishment of a common goal.

☼ **Individual Accountability**—Every member of the group is responsible for demonstrating learning related to the task.

☼ **Face-to-Face Interaction**—Students should be in close proximity with one another so they can dialogue about the task at hand.

☼ **Social Skills**—Students must learn skills to enhance trust, conflict management, leadership, decision making, and communication.

☼ **Processing**—Group members need to assess the results of their collaboration as well as the process of collaborating.

Cooperative learning begins with developing the **social** norms of *inclusion* (participating, listening, and reflecting), *influence* (valuing diversity, thinking constructively, making decisions, resolving conflict), and *community* (solving problems, working together, assessing progress, celebrating achievement).

Another important component to cooperative learning is **academic** learning. For a lesson to be a true *cooperative learning* experience rather than just *grouping*, it must highlight both a social skill *and* an academic skill or concept. For example, a lesson where students meet in groups to learn about one another's favorite things is simply grouping—there is no academic OR social skill or concept emphasized. If, during the same activity, students are asked to focus on the social skill of listening and evaluate how they listen as a group, the students are practicing social skills. Take that same lesson and go one step further by having students apply what they have learned about matrices to create a matrix for comparing and contrasting their favorite things within the group, and you've added the academic component. Students are responsible for working together and practicing listening skills (social) to use a problem-solving strategy (academic).

Tips for Managing Grouped Activities

☼ Start off the year with small groups, perhaps just pairs. When I moved to a brand-new school, the students came to me from highly traditional backgrounds. On the first day of school, I asked the students to complete an activity in groups of four—it was a mess! They hadn't been trained in how to work together and had no idea how to cooperate to achieve a goal. I rewrote my lesson plans for the next few weeks to include lessons on cooperating. I started with pairs, then moved to trios, then finally up to five students (never more) in a group. I also spent more time on team-building and cooperative skills.

☼ Arrange your room so it is conducive to group work. Provide spaces where teams can have privacy during their work.

☼ Establish a signal that you will use to get their attention, then teach the procedure for listening.

☼ Introduce a "talking stick" to help groups have one person speak at a time. You can use a tongue depressor labeled with a picture of a mouth, a cartoon speech bubble, or other synonym for "talk." Whoever is holding the talking stick is the only one who can talk. Of course, you will have to teach students how to share the stick so everyone has an opportunity to talk. It also helps to practice attentive listening, where children learn to use eye contact, to give full attention, and to affirm that the speaker is being heard through nonverbals and verbals alike. Attentive listening requires that the listener actually listen, rather than offer comments and opinions while the speaker talks.

☼ Establish group roles to help students recognize they are an essential part of the group, meeting their need to connect, contribute, and feel capable. Some helpful group roles include Speaker, Recorder, Materials Manager, Environmental Engineer, Turn Monitor, Encourager, Noise Monitor, Time Keeper, and Work Checker. Students must be trained in the roles so they know what to do. Initially, you will have to assign group roles and review the responsibilities of each role every time your students work in groups. As the year progresses, students may begin to select roles automatically. Try to rotate group roles on a regular basis, so each child has the chance to try new roles. You may want to write the roles on three- by five-inch cards and distribute them to the students randomly so they learn a variety of roles. Some primary teachers opt for putting the roles on necklaces for the children to wear during cooperative-learning activities.

Once again, talk to other teachers at your site or visit some classrooms that are engaging in group work. You will learn from the successes and failures of others!

The "Materials Manager" is responsible for getting all the supplies for the group.

"We all shine with our own small light. Together we blaze like the sun."

—Author unknown

☼ Encourage groups to solve as many of their problems as possible without teacher intervention. The students will benefit by experiencing natural and logical consequences on their own. First, you will need to teach the students skills and strategies to solve problems and get questions answered. Let them know that they are capable of managing their own groups, and in time they will learn to rely on one another.

☼ Use group work time to observe and ask questions for teaching and evaluation purposes. When students work with their peers, you will see a new side to them. Their strengths and challenges become highly apparent in group situations.

☼ Ask each student to sign a project before turning it in to signify that each student did his or her best and that the project is ready to be graded. If you are looking for proof of individual effort in cooperative assignments involving writing or drawing, consider having each child use a different colored marker on the project so you can recognize individual contributions.

☼ Take a few minutes to process group sessions. Ask the students to reflect on questions such as "What went well in the group?" "What was difficult about working together?" "What will you do the same (or differently) next time you work with the group?" "What did you learn by working with the group?" "What did you contribute to the group?" "Which cooperative skill did your group use?" You may ask students to fill out a survey to help them process these questions.

Teamwork Test

Name __Robin__   Date __December 10__

I helped my group.	☺	😐	☹
My group helped me.	☺	😐	☹
My group shared.	☺	😐	☹
My group took turns.	☺	😐	☹
My group worked hard.	☺	😐	☹

The best thing about my group is:

they are fun to work with.

Something my group needs to improve is:

sharing supplies—some kids hog them all.

Teaching Strategies and Learning Activities

Sometimes teachers find one strategy that works, such as whole-group direct instruction, and use it with all their lessons. It takes effort and research to employ various strategies that will help your students process new information in many ways, but using various strategies is well worth it because the time and effort invested help all students reach their potential. Below are six of my favorite thinking strategies that can be used across all subject areas.

ReQuest—*Reciprocal Questioning* or *Stump the Teacher*
(GRADES K–4)

When I find that I am asking all the questions, I switch to ReQuest during a topic study to get the students thinking. This strategy requires grade-level reading material (preferably nonfiction—the short articles in *Scholastic News* magazines are perfect) and a teacher who is willing to hand over the classroom reins to the students. The teacher's function is to model good questioning behavior, to provide feedback to students about their questions, and to help students establish purposes for independently completing a reading.

☼ Both the students and the teacher begin by reading the title of the selection and silently reading one common segment (perhaps a paragraph) of the selection. Allow younger students to read the passage out loud as a whole group after first reading silently, or simply use the passage as a Read Aloud.

☼ The teacher puts the text for the reading aside and students ask the teacher questions based on the information in the passage. Students may occasionally ask questions beyond the knowledge and comprehension levels. In this case, determine with your students a fair way of assessing whether or not answers can be counted as "correct."

☼ Allow three to five questions per passage. If a student asks a question that the teacher can't answer, the student has "stumped the teacher" and gets to be the "teacher" for the next segment.

☼ Continue reading the text one passage at a time; then allow students to question the "teacher."

☼ This strategy can be adapted by having students read the selection in small groups and make up one question per passage for another group to answer cooperatively.

	Body Covering	Method of Travel	Babies Born or Hatched	Warm- or Cold-Blooded
Mammal			born alive	
Bird		fly	hatch from egg	
Fish	scales			
Reptile		crawl		cold

The matrix helps students organize what they know about a topic.

Matrix (GRADES 2–4)

A matrix is a grid that charts information in a way that is easily and quickly interpreted. Students can use this strategy to:

☼ organize information

☼ identify what they know and what they don't know

☼ solve problems

☼ examine relationships between and among ideas

Teach students how to read a table or chart found in a nonfiction book so they can become familiar with the skills needed to create a matrix. Use a matrix before (pre-assessment), during (note-taking sheet), or after (post-assessment) studying a topic.

Provide students with a grid of intersecting columns and rows. Label the rows with topics and the columns with generic characteristics of the topics. Then, ask students to fill in any information they already know about the specific characteristics of the topics and to conduct research to complete the matrix. Finally, discuss the completed matrix with the class, keying in on how the topics are alike and different, how the topics are related, or how to use the information to solve problems.

You can create a matrix on butcher paper to use as a whole-class exercise or review.

K-W-L (GRADES K–4)

The K-W-L (Know-Wonder-Learned) accesses prior knowledge, helps students set goals for their learning, and gives the teacher a way to assess content-area learning. Use it before and after a unit of study.

☼ *Before teaching a topic or concept,* ask students what they *know or think they know* about it and have them list their thoughts in the first column. Then have the students list any questions they have about the topic or concept in the second column.

☼ *During the lesson,* ask students to review whether or not the information in the first column was correct, if any of their questions were answered, and if they learned anything. This information gets placed in the third column.

You may choose to do the K-W-L as a whole group on a piece of butcher paper, which can be saved for future review. The K-W-L works for younger children when done orally or in pictures. When doing the K-W-L individually, have students fold a piece of paper into thirds and label the first column "Know," the second "Wonder," and the third "Learned."

I created a K-W-L bulletin board in my class. Students brainstormed what they knew about the topic as a whole group on a chart and placed it on the first section of the bulletin board. During free time, students wrote questions about the topic and tacked them to the board in the middle section. As students discovered answers, they removed the questions, wrote the answers under the questions, and placed them on the final third of the bulletin board. When the unit concluded, I bound the questions and answers with a ring clip to make a mini-book of knowledge that the students could check out from the class library.

The interactive K-W-L bulletin board can be used all year long.

We Know	We Wonder	We Learned
Rocks	**Q.** What rocks are valuable?	**A.** Silver, gold, and concrete
• Rocks are hard.	**Q.** Why are rocks hard?	
• Rocks come in different colors.	**Q.** How does a volcano make rocks?	**A.** I learned not to throw rocks.
• Rocks have minerals in them.	**Q.** How are rocks made?	
• There are lots of kinds of rocks.	**Q.** What makes rocks red?	**A.** Iron and water
• Rocks are made in different ways.		

A jigsaw supports students as they become "experts" in one portion of a topic.

Jigsaw (GRADES 1–4)

A Jigsaw is one way to get through a great deal of material in a short amount of time. It employs peer discussion to help each student become an "expert" on one portion of information, then teach it to the others in the group. Use a Jigsaw before or during instruction on the topic.

☼ Form groups of equal numbers. These are the "home" groups. Number off within groups.

☼ Establish norms for group behavior (see page 141).

☼ Like numbers from each group get together to read one part of an article or story (each group of like numbers has a different part to read, so they become experts in that part). The expert group decides how they will summarize their part of the article or story for the others in their home group who have not read that part.

☼ Individuals return to their original home groups where each person takes no more than three minutes to share the essence of the part of the article or story his or her group read. The home group then constructs a summary of its collective learnings.

Jigsaw

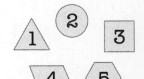

Home Group

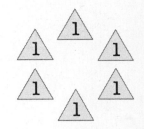

Expert Group

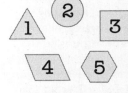

Home Group

Venn Diagram (GRADES 1–4)

Use a Venn diagram at any stage of a lesson to help students compare and contrast two topics, characters, people, objects, or concepts. You can do this as a whole class or students can do it individually.

☼ Draw two overlapping circles on a piece of paper.

☼ Label each circle with a different topic, character, person, object, or concept.

☼ Write how the two are alike in the center where the circles overlap.

☼ Write how they are different on the appropriate side of the two circles.

A Venn diagram is a graphic organizer for comparing and contrasting.

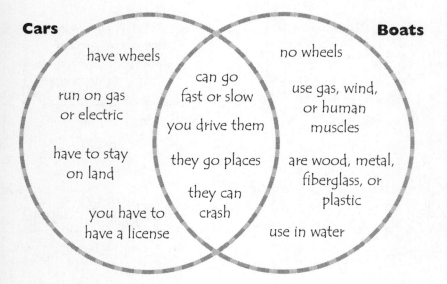

Cars
have wheels
run on gas or electric
have to stay on land
you have to have a license

can go fast or slow
you drive them
they go places
they can crash

Boats
no wheels
use gas, wind, or human muscles
are wood, metal, fiberglass, or plastic
use in water

Younger children can draw pictures or do this as a whole-group exercise. You can even create a floor Venn diagram. Have students wearing jeans stand in one circle and students with brown hair stand in the other circle. Students who meet both criteria stand where the circles overlap.

Once older students have mastered the two-way Venn diagram, they may try a three-way Venn diagram by adding a third circle which enables them to compare and contrast three topics, characters, people, objects, or concepts.

List-Group-Label (GRADES K–4)

Use this at all stages of instruction to help students see relationships between topics and skills.

☼ The teacher or students may select the topic or skill to be studied and write it on the board.

☼ Students brainstorm words or phrases relating to the topic or skill. The teacher records their responses on large strips of paper (one idea per strip) and randomly tapes them on the board.

☼ Students group the words or phrases that go together. If there are additional words to be taught, the teacher writes the new words on strips and the students decide where the words belong. Form a new category for words that don't fit in the established groups.

☼ Students name or label each group of words or phrases.

This strategy can also be done with pictures for younger students.

Peruse *Brain Compatible Classrooms* by Robin Fogarty for more effective strategies, and *Designing Brain Compatible Learning* by Terrence Parry and Gayle Gregory for some great graphic organizers.

Learning Activities

To help students get the most mileage out of classroom experiences, a variety of instructional activities can be used to assist them in processing new information. These activities can be used at most grade levels, across the curriculum, and with almost any topic to integrate content areas. The following are some of my favorite activities designed to involve students in their learning.

✧ **Graphic Organizers for Story Elements**—There are many types of graphic organizers. Ones like the example at right can be used to assess reading comprehension, develop an understanding of story elements as a whole-group lesson, or help students organize their thoughts and generate vocabulary for their writing. I find that amazing stories are written when students use organizers as an opportunity to rehearse for writing.

✧ **ABC Book**—After conducting research on any topic, students can brainstorm ideas for an ABC book to show what they have learned. Assign letters to students; then give each child a piece of construction paper on which to write and illustrate one idea to put in the book. An ABC book on Red Rock Canyon might include pages such as: "A is for Anasazi—the ancient ones," "B is for Boulder—there are large boulders of sandstone at Red Rock," "C is for Canyon—Ice Box Canyon gets cold breezes." Bind the book to keep in the class library. You may also choose to make copies of it for the students to use during reading instruction—they are always more interested when they're reading their own or their peers' writing.

My class created an innovation on the fun alphabet book On Market Street. ▶

Graphic Organizer for Reading and Writing Fiction

Name _____   Title _____   Date _____

Plot (What, Why, How?)

_____
Type of Story

Beginning

◆ What is the problem?

◆ Why is there a problem?

◆ How does the beginning make you feel?

Middle

◆ What are two important things that happen in the middle?

1. _____

2. _____

End

◆ How is the problem solved?

◆ How does the ending make you feel?

▲

These graphic organizers can be used after reading or before writing a story.

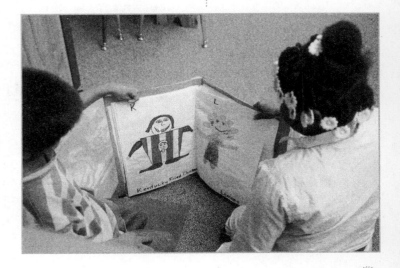

☼ **You Were There**—Another fun way to help students process research is to have them "time travel" to a famous event or location, then "become" news reporters and characters. Journalists can interview participants or observe them role-playing the action, then write a newspaper article about the event.

☼ **Stage It**—Students can demonstrate comprehension of a fictional story by turning it into a play or choral reading. Teach them how to write a script then set them loose—you'll be amazed at their creativity! One of my favorite third-grade activities was to have small groups transform different chapters from *The Adventures of Spider*, by J. Arkhurst, into scripts. For backdrops, they drew scenery on overhead transparencies (or the excess fused-laminating film that teachers usually throw away) with permanent markers. To show the backdrops, I placed the overhead projector behind the action, facing a large white sheet. The projector showed the backdrop as large as life on the sheet. It took much less time (and wore out fewer markers or crayons) than creating backdrops on butcher paper.

☼ **Talk Show**—Have students create a talk show featuring the characters from a book they've read. Children prepare questions and answers that offer insight into the characters they are portraying, demonstrating comprehension of character traits. You'll have some exceptional "Oprahs" or "Geraldos" in your class! Let them create a microphone out of a toilet paper roll and really get into the role of host. They can even involve the audience.

☼ **Cartoon It**—After reading a story with a clear sequence, have students divide a piece of paper into 4 to 12 squares, depending upon their grade level and/or the number of events in the story. Ask them to illustrate the important events from the book in sequence using a comic-strip format. You can teach them that whatever goes in the bubble of a comic strip is a direct quote and requires quotation marks when written in a book.

☼ **Picture This**—Students illustrate and label an event from the beginning, middle, and end of a book on a paper folded into thirds (also known as a "burrito fold" in "kid language"; folding a paper in half lengthwise is a "hot dog fold"; folding it in half the short way is a "taco fold"; folding it in fourths is a "hamburger fold"). Older students can write a paragraph summarizing what happened in each part of the story.

My students taught me easily understood language for folding paper in a variety of ways. ▼

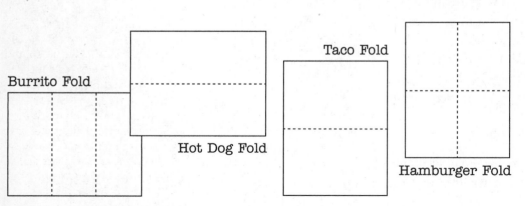

Burrito Fold

Hot Dog Fold

Taco Fold

Hamburger Fold

Where Is It?—Students brainstorm information about the setting from a fictional story, then draw a map of what the area could look like. *The Hobbit*, by J. R. R. Tolkien, has several excellent examples of fictional maps that look real. *Roxaboxen*, by Alice McLerran and Barbara Cooney, and *The Lion, the Witch, and the Wardrobe*, by C. S. Lewis, are good books to use with this activity.

Board Games—*Jumanji*, by Chris van Allsburg, is a good vehicle for teaching children how to make board games. After reading any book, students can create their own board game that hits the high points of the action.

Reproduction—Students copy the exact text from a story, then illustrate it according to their understanding of the text. You can also print the text on a mini-book format, make a copy for each student to illustrate, and send the mini-books home for student practice.

Innovation—Students rewrite a story, changing one or more components. To innovate a fairy tale, tell it from a different character's point of view (*The True Story of the Three Little Pigs*), change the qualities of the characters (*The Frog Prince, Continued*), change the setting (*The Three Little Javelinas*), or modernize the story (*The Principal's New Clothes*). Predictable books are excellent for innovations—a classic example is to turn *Brown Bear, Brown Bear, What Do You See?* into "Children, Children, What Do You See?" as a first-week kindergarten project.

Directed Reading-Writing-Thinking Activity—Read a story to the students, stopping in key places to ask them to write or draw what they think will happen next. Give them just one or two minutes for each prediction; then have a few children share what they thought would happen before moving on with the story. Older students can write their predictions, exchange papers at each stopping point and react to one another's ideas on paper. Involve everyone and model appreciation for each child's contribution and unique thinking.

Research Writing—Here's a great idea on how to assist students in research writing without letting them plagiarize. Have the students brainstorm the general topics others might want to know about the research topic. For example, if they are studying an animal, categories might include appearance, habitat, enemies, family, and interesting habits; if they are studying a country, categories might include location, people, plant life, animal life, and celebrations. Students choose three categories and write them across the top of a Data Chart (see page 150). Then they find three sources for information (you can also make a Data Chart with two sources) and write the bibliographies on the back of the Data Chart. As they read through a source, they write a few words to help them remember what they've read in the appropriate column—there isn't room to copy entire sentences. After their research is completed, they are ready to turn the brief notes into meaningful

Tony Stead has recently published an excellent book, *Is That a Fact? Teaching Nonfiction Writing K–3*, for teachers who want their students to write nonfiction effectively. It's hot off the press and can be ordered from Mondo Publications.

Data Chart

Name _____Carol_____   Topic _____Canaries_____

	Appearance	Eating Habits	Fun Facts
SOURCE 1	all colors (yellow, brown, green, orange, white, gray)	seeds ◆ canary grass ◆ millet ◆ poppy ◆ thistle	When a boy likes a girl he feeds her, then they build a nest and lay three to six eggs
SOURCE 2	three kinds of feathers—fluffy down, long flight feathers, body contour feathers	◆ seeds and bugs ◆ they eat a lot	Baby canaries are naked when they hatch, but their feathers grow in two weeks.
SOURCE 3	◆ two feet with four claws each (three front and one back) ◆ some have crests like hair on their heads	seeds, marigolds, hard-boiled eggs, Kale, cucumbers	Boy canaries sing better songs than girl canaries. They can be very loud.

sentences and paragraphs, which have been roughly organized in the Data Chart columns. Data Charts can be used successfully in grades two through five, and sometimes even the end of first grade, if students are working in mixed-ability groups to do the research.

I was thrilled when a colleague shared the idea of a Data Chart with me—no more plagiarism!

Assessment

In the third section of this book, you began to conduct student assessments and worked out a grading system. Let's continue our exploration of assessment. Assessment is collecting data to provide an array of evidence, while evaluation is appraising what has been collected. Teachers use formative and summative assessments, along with student self-assessment, to measure learning and to make informed decisions on instruction. Each type of assessment has a different purpose and application.

☼ **Formative assessments** are ongoing, focus on a few specific skills or concepts at a time, and may be formal or informal. They assist teachers with designing instruction to meet the individual needs of their students more effectively. They also provide students (and their parents) with measured feedback on their progress. EXAMPLES: teacher observation, checklists, teacher-made tests, performance assessment, project assessment, and questioning techniques.

☼ **Summative assessments** are one-time, formal measures covering a variety of skills and concepts. Their results are generally tabulated long after the actual test has been taken, so they are most useful for helping teachers evaluate the effectiveness of their daily instruction over a period of time. EXAMPLE: norm-referenced tests such as the TerraNova, which is administered in order to compare students across the country.

☼ **Self-assessments** help children recognize their own learning and provide them with a point of reference against which they can judge their progress. Students may self-assess their academic skills, their social skills, or even their behavior. EXAMPLES: self-correction, self-selection, and portfolio development and analysis.

Observing Students

Sedere, the origin of the word *assessment*, means "to sit beside." You will gain valuable information about your students by "sitting beside" them, watching them and talking to them the first week of school. I consistently gained a great deal of insight into my students by watching them at work *and* at play. You'll also need to assess your students' skills and knowledge in math, reading, and writing. I'm sure you'll notice a great variety of levels in your class regardless of the grade you teach; for example, all fourth graders don't necessarily have a solid grasp of addition or subtraction, and some won't be ready for multiplication or division.

In observing children, watch for frustration (the child is unable to do the work independently) and boredom (the student is not challenged by the content). When the content is higher than the child's level, the teacher must adapt whole-group activities so all students can participate and gain something from the lesson. These students must also be pulled out for small-group lessons based on needs. If, for example, the majority of your students are ready for double-digit multiplication, but you notice that four students still have great difficulty with basic multiplication facts, you will need to do extensive work with those four. Don't remediate the whole class, as most of your students will be bored. Don't teach the new concept without the prerequisite skills in place, as the four students will be frustrated. It's time for small-group, needs-based instruction: Work with the four students in need on gaining an understanding of the basic concept. Make sure the students you aren't working with at the time have meaningful work to do, perhaps expanding on what they already know about the concept. With boredom, small groups based on needs may be the answer here. Always have something meaningful and appropriately challenging prepared for students who finish independent work early. I gave students three choices: read, write, or make up math problems for a partner to solve. Students can also peer-tutor others who need help; their own understanding will deepen as they help others.

As you begin teaching new content, remember that just because you've taught something, it doesn't mean your students have learned it. Each school day offers numerous opportunities to assess student understanding and progress. Some assessments will be informal quick checks or observations, while others will be more detailed and formal. The goal of any assessment is to gain a clearer picture of what an individual has learned, the way he or she learned it, and how he or she uses what has been learned. Keep these ideas in mind as you assess your students' learning:

☼ Glean information from each student's daily experiences and interactions.

☼ Use data from tests to supplement your observations.

☼ Watch the process children go through to master skills, concepts, or content.

☼ Ask students to think aloud for you so you can probe their understanding of content and strategies.

☼ Build student portfolios to record performance benchmarks during the year.

☼ Use every possible source of information to create a rich tapestry of assessment enabling you to determine appropriate instruction for each student.

Let's look at a few ways to gather information about the learning that is going on in your classroom so you can take steps to reach every child in your class, without letting a single student go unnoticed or unserved.

Gathering Information...

Informal **observation** ("kid-watching") of students working alone, in groups, or during whole-group instruction can give you valuable information about students' progress, understanding, strengths and challenges, cooperation, study habits, and attitude. There are many ways to record observations you make. Use sticky notes to jot down your thoughts and then post them on a chart with your students' names, prepare a **checklist** of things you want to look for as students work, or keep a folder with records of your observations written on self-stick labels or sheets of paper. *EXAMPLE: You're concerned about the study habits of a student. Throughout the day, make notes of the student's attitude during various class activities, times when she is on- or off-task, which students she works with best, how long she can maintain attention to non-academic activities (e.g., P.E., art, music, games at recess). After collecting this context-rich information, you may have a better idea of how to help the child improve her study habits or how to adapt your instruction to better involve her.*

Have you ever known a child to memorize a fact or an answer without first understanding a concept? It happens all the time in math! A big challenge for me as a third-grade teacher was convincing my students that even though they had memorized their multiplication tables at home during the summer after second grade, we had to go back and relearn what multiplication actually meant. Conducting **interviews** with individual students can help you get beyond surface memorization to check true understanding. *EXAMPLE: To assess understanding of the concept of addition, don't simply give a worksheet of 20 addition problems and use the grade to determine comprehension. While students need written practice with addition facts, a worksheet alone will not necessarily let you see into the mind of the child. Sit down with children individually or in small groups and ask them to give you examples of real-life situations where addition would be used; have them draw a picture of an addition problem and tell you about it; ask students how they know their answer is correct; or ask students if they can think of a general rule that applies to addition.*

Questioning is similar to the process of interviewing, but is more informal. As students work on an assignment, circulate to ask individuals questions relating to their work. *EXAMPLE: After teaching a lesson on reading for information followed by an assignment to read a selection and answer questions, ask students things such as, "What information do you need to know?" "Where will you get that information?" "Can you tell me more?" "What is the most interesting part of the reading?" "What have you learned?" Help students do Think Alouds by asking them to talk you through what they are doing.*

Self-assessment is a valuable skill for students to learn. Give students opportunities to assess their efforts and attitudes regularly. Students can do this through questionnaires, journaling, and checklists. *EXAMPLE: Following a cooperative learning activity, students could fill out a questionnaire asking them to rate their performance on statements, such as "I helped my group," "My group helped me," "My group shared," and "I took turns with the others in my group." They could write in their journal about the most important thing they learned from the activity. Students could also create a list of skills they "can-do": "I can capitalize at the beginning of a sentence," "I can read words with short /a/."*

A **conference** is a dialogue with an individual student. A conference may center around reading, writing, math, content areas, or goal setting. Many teachers structure their day so they have time to meet with individual students in a 10- to 15-minute conference setting every week or two, depending on the type of conference. *EXAMPLE: To assess progress in writing, meet with students individually on a regular basis. If you have your students write every day, keep their work in a folder or notebook in chronological order. During the conference, have the student read aloud something she has written, and ask what she likes best about the writing. Tell her what you like best about the writing, then select* one *skill or concept to focus on for the conference. If the student is having trouble using descriptive words in the story or report, ask the student how she could tell more about the main character so that the audience could draw a picture from the description, finding more exciting words to substitute for overused words such as "nice," "good," "bad," and "mean." Have her draw a detailed portrait of the main character to assist with a detailed description, or help her complete a senses web, describing what she might see, hear, smell, taste, and feel in the setting. After gaining a more complete picture herself, the student then goes back through the piece and inserts words that will better describe the setting.*

A **performance assessment** shows what students can do by performing a task related to a skill or concept that has been taught in class. *EXAMPLE: Having learned about sedimentary rocks, students could sort rock samples into sedimentary and non-sedimentary. After learning how to take notes for research, have them actually conduct research on a self-selected topic.*

Sometimes you will prefer to assess student progress with a **teacher-made test**. Create a few questions or tasks that get at the heart of the skill or concept. Tests can be of a traditional format (essay, multiple choice, true or false, short answer), performance-based, or tied to the multiple intelligences.

For ideas on doing writing conferences with children, try *Write On: A Conference Approach to Writing* (Parry and Hornsby) or *Let's Write* (Areglado and Dill).

Record Keeping and Reporting

Portfolios, rubrics, and progress reports are three ways to track student progress and show it to parents and school personnel.

Portfolios

For more on portfolios, check out *Portfolio Assessment for Your Whole Language Classroom* by Julia Jasmine.

A portfolio is an accumulation of student work that can accompany the student from grade to grade or be sent home at the end of the school year. To evaluate student progress effectively, you must have a good understanding of what each piece of student work displays in terms of learning so the portfolio grade is meaningful, useful, and easily explained to parents and students.

Three types of portfolios are:

☼ **The Collection Portfolio:** This portfolio contains a wide variety of student work completed over a period of time. It could include a piece of writing taken through the entire writing process, writing samples showing different parts of the process, writing from content-area assignments, writing rubrics attached to a piece of writing, a daily journal or writing notebook, notes from student interviews or conferences, reading inventories or checklists, book reports or reviews, taped recordings of oral reading, video tapes of skits, photographs of projects or activities, mathematics checklists, math problem-solving Think Alouds, and student explanations of criteria for selection.

☼ **Student Showcase Portfolio:** This portfolio includes carefully selected artifacts (chosen by teacher or student) that represent the student's best work or work that shows growth over time and is intended to be publicly displayed (at open houses, parent-teacher conferences, report-card time, or once a month). The Student Showcase could include student reflections on the selections and student self-assessments.

☼ **Assessment Portfolio:** This portfolio contains teacher-selected items, including student work documenting tests and test scores, anecdotal notes of observations and conferences, and records of other assessment tools, such as interest inventories, student evaluations, and goal-setting forms. This type of portfolio is typically used by the teacher to inform students and parents rather than for public display.

You may choose to use one, two, or all three of these types of portfolios, depending on your needs and the requirements of your school. Items from the Collection Portfolio can be included in the Selection Portfolio and the Assessment Portfolio. Consider your record-keeping needs and the purpose of each portfolio carefully before you begin collecting documents.

Creating portfolios is easy. The portfolio container can be as simple as folded construction paper or a manila folder. You can also use pocket folders, three-ring notebooks, or even empty cereal boxes! Portfolios may be created for any subject and integrated or kept separately. They should be easily accessible to students, teachers, and parents for quick filing and reference.

Grading of portfolio contents and other student work is a highly personal task; each school and even each teacher approaches it differently. Check with your administrator for site grading guidelines. Also, locate a copy of the report card for your grade level early in the fall. The report card will be very helpful in setting up a grade book and determining which grading scale(s) is required.

These portfolios were made from empty cereal boxes covered with contact paper. ▶

Rubrics

Rubrics allow teachers to put a number to the knowledge and skill levels for individual children. They break skills and concepts into increments for easy evaluation. You can use rubrics for a specific assignment or to evaluate a student's overall performance in a content area.

This rubric was developed for a primary classroom. ▶

Selects a Variety of Literature for Independent or Partner Reading

4 consistently selects a variety of genres for independent or partner reading

3 usually stays within one genre for independent or partner reading

2 usually reads the same book(s) for independent or partner reading

1 does not voluntarily select literature for independent or partner reading

 located a super tutorial on how to develop rubrics at **www.teach-nology.com/tutorials/teaching/rubrics/develop**. I also found a "rubric bank" (a collection of rubrics for each subject area) on the Chicago Public Schools web site. Go to **intranet.cps.k12.il.us/Assessments/Ideas_and_Rubrics/Rubric_Bank/rubric_bank.html**—it's a gold mine!

Progress Reports

To be effective in reporting progress, do it often and as positively as possible. A weekly progress report helps parents not be surprised by the actual report cards. As with student conferences, select just one area in need of improvement. Occasionally, I have the students themselves identify the area to be improved and write it on the weekly progress report for self-assessment purposes (see pages 186–188).

Test-Taking Strategies...

We want all of our students to feel successful with standardized tests and assessments of any kind. While we mustn't teach to the test, there are ways to help students become better test takers:

☼ Teach students general strategies for making a test less stressful; they might try visualizing success, relaxing breathing, and so on. Help them understand that fearing tests makes it harder to think.

☼ Don't imply that tests have anything to do with student grades or passing to the next grade at the end of the year; children can be world-class worriers!

☼ Teach students that you don't expect perfection and that you just want them to *do* their personal best, not *be* the best.

☼ Demystify tests by frequently practicing skills and concepts in a test-like format. Many children do poorly on tests simply because they are unfamiliar with the format. Give them opportunities during the year to experience the process of answering many types of questions.

☼ Give students frequent chances to practice following directions.

☼ Assist students in understanding the nature of timed tests. Have them close their eyes (stand on one leg, run in place) for what they think is one minute (or five minutes). Give them an opportunity to compare their estimate with the real amount of time. Occasionally have students answer questions in a timed format so they develop strategies for not wasting time.

☼ A few days before a major test, I send out a letter to parents explaining the nature of the test, when it will occur, and how to help at home by making sure that their child:

◆ gets a good night's sleep before the day of the test
◆ eats a good breakfast (with very little sugar) the morning of the test
◆ wears comfortable clothes appropriate for school
◆ has parental support and understanding if he or she is anxious or upset
◆ doesn't receive pressure in the form of threats or rewards attached to test results

☼ Dividing the test into small parts to accommodate for your students' attention spans is highly effective. While it is tempting to try to get through some tests in a few sittings, especially in the intermediate grades, your students will be better able to focus on the test if they have ample breaks and opportunities for movement between sections.

As you prepare your students for taking a test, talk to your administrator for guidelines on how testing is handled at your site so you will be well versed in testing practices.

Students With Special Needs

Numerous special-needs programs are available for students throughout the country. Many schools are able to provide services for:

- students who are gifted and/or academically talented
- students with learning disabilities
- students who need extra support in reading
- students who have difficulty with speech
- students who are English-language learners (ESL or bilingual classrooms)
- students who need counseling
- students who have great behavior challenges
- students who are living in poverty
- homeless students

Services may be available at some sites on a part-time basis or require a referral for off-site services. Find out which programs are in place in your district and what their goals are.

With so many support programs, it sometimes seems as though your classroom has a revolving door, with students leaving the room for various special classes at all times of the day. It is a great challenge to maintain a structure while remaining flexible to accommodate the needs of all students.

Assistance for students with special needs takes a variety of forms. As an alternative to traditional pullout programs, many schools now operate under the Cooperative/Consultative (C/C) model, which was designed to include students in the regular classroom. The C/C model provides remedial strategies within the regular classroom setting to students who require minimal special-education services and provides methods, materials, and resources for regular education teachers to assist in meeting the needs of students. While pullout programs may result in isolation, labels and stigmas, anxiety, competitiveness, or feeling unwelcome, inclusion is intended to promote community, acceptance, friendship, hospitality, and cooperation. The C/C model that was in place when I taught third grade involved the resource room teacher coming to my class to support my students with learning disabilities during regular class activities. A bonus to this was that the teacher could also observe students about whom I was concerned but hadn't yet been identified as having a learning disability. No matter how special services are offered at your school, enlist the special-needs teachers in improving the quality of your instruction and behavior management. They may be willing to share resources with you or even model lessons if you only ask.

The Diverse Classroom

As a new teacher, you may be struggling with the complexity of teaching a highly diverse student population. To create a learning environment that is accepting of differences, it is important to recognize and appreciate the special talents that each child brings to your classroom. The first lesson to learn is that every student CAN DO something well. This is one of the reasons the theory of multiple intelligences appeals to me. It brings light to the many abilities that students can have beyond the 3 R's—readin', writin', and 'rithmetic. Applaud the strengths of each of your students—artistic ability, skill in physical activities, the ability to tell a good joke, a sensitivity to music, a connection with nature, the ability to de-escalate an argument. Find out what students' interests are and designate them as the "experts" on their favorite topic.

Planning and delivering instruction for a diverse group of students is challenging to all teachers; however, experienced teachers have a larger "bag of tricks" from which to draw. Some activities are appropriate for students at all levels. For example, every student can express himself or herself in writing—maybe not with correct spelling or even with actual words, but expression is the key. Even children who don't possess the physical skills for holding a pencil can dictate their thoughts to others or work with a computer. Every student can journal on a daily basis, and the teacher can facilitate growth by giving feedback on one skill at a time.

Other activities require adaptations to meet the needs of individual students. Below is an example of how some teachers think when modifying lessons for students with special needs.

☼ Start by asking yourself, "What are the prerequisite skills and concepts involved in the lesson?" The answer will be the standard against which you evaluate the ease or difficulty of the lesson. If the child has not mastered the skills or doesn't understand the concepts, attempting to do the activity as originally planned will be very frustrating. Conversely, if the child has already mastered the content, why not let him or her continue to learn in a different way?

☼ Then ask, "Can the student complete the lesson as planned and at the same level as his or her peers?" or "Will the student benefit from taking part in the lesson?"

   ◈ If the answer is "yes," then you need not modify the lesson.

   ◈ If the answer is "no," then begin asking, "What can I change so the student will be successfully included in the learning activities?" I create adaptations for students who are performing below the standard and students who are performing above the standard.

How to Reach and Teach All Students in the Inclusive Classroom by Sandra Rief and Julie Heimburge is one resource you shouldn't be without! Even if you don't have students with exceptionalities in your classroom, you will learn a great deal about teaching from this guide. I purchased it secondhand through Amazon.com and was pleased both with the discount and the condition of the book.

What Can I Change?	Example—Student Performing Below Standard	Example—Student Performing Above Standard
Same activity at different level	Sort easier words	Sort more advanced words
Same activity with different expectations	Sort 10 rather than 20 words	Sort all 20 words in less than 2 minutes
Same activity with different materials	Sort pictures rather than words	Sort words on the classroom computer
Same activity with peer or adult assistance	Sort all 20 words with the help of the teacher's aide	N/A
Different activity at same level	Draw a picture of each word	Use all 20 words in a story with a beginning, middle, and end
Different parallel activity	Learn how to use the spell-checker on a word-processing program	Research the origin of complex words
Different unrelated activity in the room	Read a book, draw a picture, work on math problems	Research a science or social studies topic of choice
Different unrelated activity in another part of school	Help the librarian, office staff, or custodian	Cross-age tutor a student from the grade below

▲ *The changes in this table were created to adapt a generic spelling lesson for which students are sorting 20 words according to spelling characteristics.*

Getting Help for Students

The process of referring students for special services can be time-consuming and sometimes frustrating. You will have to locate information from the school office and provide specific information and insights based on your work with the student. Your job will be easier if you maintain good records and keep them organized so you can locate them at a moment's notice.

One important aspect of getting additional assistance for students is documenting what you have tried and how well, if at all, it worked. When meeting with an assistance team, be prepared with checklists, student work, records of parent conferences, and concrete examples of how you implemented an intervention, how long you tried it, what you noticed, and what you did next. Without documentation, efforts at getting the assistance your students need can take more time than you anticipated. Here is one of my favorite organizers for collecting information on students whom you wish to refer for special assistance. It works for academic and behavior issues.

Numerous interventions have been developed to assist teachers in dealing with behavioral and academic problems in the classroom. Here are a few interventions you might wish to try if what you're doing now isn't working with a student.

If you are searching for additional ways to intervene in specific situations, you will want to locate a copy of the *Teacher's Resource Guide* by Dr. Steven McCarney (previous versions were entitled *PRIM—Pre-referral Intervention Manual*). You will find 20 to 40 suggestions each for intervening in hundreds of behavioral (tattling, fighting, talking out of turn) and academic (unable to follow directions for activities, not finishing work) difficulties!

Material and Environmental Interventions...

☼ use high-interest, low-level materials

☼ modify the length of the assignment

☼ allow additional time to complete the assignment

☼ use manipulatives, models, and realia (actual objects)

☼ break the task into small steps

☼ adjust instruction to the student's preferred learning style (visual, auditory, kinesthetic)

☼ give the student choices in how to demonstrate mastery of the material (reciting rather than writing, drawing, building a model)

☼ change the student's seating (near teacher, close to the board, by a wall) or the overall room arrangement

☼ use a timer

☼ use adaptive equipment (tape recorder, computer, pencil grip)

Interpersonal Interventions...

☼ provide one-on-one teacher time

☼ solicit assistance from an adult volunteer, peer tutor, or cross-age tutor

☼ ask for directed parent help at home

☼ schedule a conference with student, parent, school counselor, and/or principal

Behavioral and Motivational Interventions...

☼ clarify rules, expectations, and procedures

☼ model the desired behavior

☼ encourage the student (see pages 83–85)

☼ reinforce appropriate responses promptly

☼ reward the student for starting, continuing, and finishing tasks (see pages 86–90)

☼ send home daily or weekly effort, achievement, and/or behavior reports

☼ create a behavior or performance contract

☼ use logical consequences (see pages 89–93)

☼ give students think time (as opposed to "time out")

Things to Think About

Key Questions for Student-Assistance Team

◆ Who is present when the behavior tends to occur? when it almost never occurs?

◆ What is going on when the behavior tends to occur? when it almost never occurs?

◆ When does the behavior tend to occur? When does it almost never occur?

◆ Where does the behavior tend to occur? almost never occur?

You have overcome so many hurdles so far this year! Celebrate your successes by writing them down. You will be amazed at how much you have actually accomplished!

The End Is Near:

Ending the Year With Style

It will seem as if you have just blinked your eyes and here it is—the last day of school. At the end of the year, keeping the momentum going through the last day of school is key. Maintain your rules, procedures, and routines so students have the structure they've come to expect from you. Make instruction exciting to ensure that students continue learning *and* have no desire to misbehave after the climax of the end-of-the-year testing. Finally, provide closure for the year so students feel complete.

Spend some time brainstorming highlights of the school year with the class. Then have students wrap up the year by writing songs, scripts, stories, or letters that explain what they have learned during the year. Share the results with students who will be coming to that grade level next year so they will get a "sneak preview" of all the excitement coming their way.

Have each student write you a letter telling what he or she liked best about your class and offering suggestions for improvement. You will cherish these letters for years to come *and* get some great ideas for next year! Hearing what your students felt about your class can be enlightening.

Take your students to visit the classrooms for the next grade. My kindergartners really enjoyed going to first grade and meeting the teachers; it took some of the nervousness out of the transition from kindergarten to first grade. The first graders even gave advice to my little ones and shared some of the neat things they got to do in first grade.

Create "thank you" cards or books for the people who keep the school running—administrators, office staff, custodian, cafeteria workers, nurse, bus drivers, teacher assistants, specialists. Deliver them as a class, complete with hugs or handshakes.

Begin removing student work from the walls, but don't tear down your room before the students leave. I know taking everything off ahead of time would save you time later, but it is so sad to face the last day of school in a bare classroom. Maybe do some of the other checkout activities first and save the dismantling of the room for the last few minutes of the last day if you want to have your students help you; they could probably find good uses at home for the butcher paper and construction paper that will be thrown away anyway. Have students pack up their materials, supplies, portfolios (if they don't stay at school), projects, and other belongings on the day *before* the last day of school. It is too hectic to wait until the last day. I bring lots of grocery sacks just in case the students forget their backpacks.

Have an awards ceremony for your students where you present each one with some type of a remembrance and a certificate. I like to get a variety of pencils from a teacher-supply store so each student's is unique and describes his or her personality or talents. Please don't leave anyone out; you can find something positive to say about every child in your class! I let the children know that the pencils are for next year, so they can remember to do their personal best in their new class; the students really cherish them.

Send home an end-of-the-year parent letter to express your appreciation of their support. Some parents dread summer as they don't know what to do with their children over a stretch of two and a half months. I like to send out a generic calendar of activities for parents to do with their children at home so the learning continues throughout the summer. The activities on the summer calendars can be adapted for year-round schedules (see pages 188–189). I've also known teachers who set up a reading program for their students over the summer; when school started up again, the children brought their reading contracts to their former teacher to receive a prize and a warm "good luck in your new class."

◀ *Have students write or draw about special times, what they learned, their friends, and plans for next year.*

Wading Through the Paperwork

This section is designed to give you some information on things you will probably need to do at the end of the year to close out your classroom. Use this list as an advance organizer to prepare yourself for what *may* come!

End of the Year: To Do and Find Out...

○ Are there any schoolwide end-of-the-year events (field day, staff vs. student softball game, awards assembly)? *If so, allow extra time in your lesson plans so you won't be rushed at the last minute.*

○ When do report cards have to be completed? Does the principal have to fill anything out or sign the final report card? Do I send report cards home with the students, do parents pick them up, or do they go into the mail? *Keep a copy of the final report card for your records and place a copy in the students' cumulative files if required.*

○ Is there paperwork that needs to be completed and placed in student files or turned in to the office staff?

○ What happens if library books or instructional materials have been lost? Do the students have to pay for them? How do I go about reordering materials that were lost?

○ Do I need to inventory and/or turn in instructional materials (books, records, tapes, CDs, slides, filmstrips, manipulatives, science kits) and teacher's guides?

○ What do I do with my lesson plans, attendance folder, and grade book?

○ Do I keep AV equipment and computers in my classroom? If there is a piece of equipment that needs servicing, what should I do?

○ Can I keep my walls decorated or do they have to be dismantled? Does the furniture need to be moved or stacked so the carpets can be cleaned or the tile waxed?

○ What do I do if something in my room needs maintenance?

○ What do I do with unclaimed report cards, student supplies, lost lunch pails, and clothing?

○ Do I need to have someone check my room before I leave?

○ Do I turn in my keys?

○ When will the building be open again so I can get ready for next year?

Full Circle: Setting Goals for Your Second Year of Successful Teaching

Your first year of teaching is over! Did you ever imagine that teaching would be such a complex career choice? Since you're still here reading this book, I know that you made it through the ups and downs and that you're ready to do it again next year. Congratulations! It's time now to look ahead to your second year of teaching.

Now that you're rested, you'll probably want to get started planning for next year. But don't do a thing until you've revisited your vision and action plan from last year.

Look back now to pages 9 through 13. Pull out your vision and action plan, have your "Celebration Journal" handy and, if you used one, your Ideas for Next Year notebook. As you reread what you expected from this year, ask yourself the following questions.

A Trip Down Memory Lane

- ☼ Which parts of my dream did I achieve?

- ☼ How do I know that I was successful in these areas?

- ☼ How did I feel when I achieved success in these areas?

- ☼ Which parts of my dream were not realized?

- ☼ How do I know that these parts of my dream didn't "come true"?

- ☼ How can I go about realizing these parts of my dream next year?

- ☼ Did the action plan work out? Were the "baby steps" effective in helping me reach my vision?

Because your dream was for your first year of teaching, you will need to update it as you prepare for your second year. So go through the process again; repeat steps 1–5 on pages 10–13 to create a vision of success for your second year of teaching. Be sure to:

☼ visualize what success looks like for you (see page 10)

☼ create an action plan that will get you there (see page 11)

☼ revisit your vision of success daily to set it in your mind (see page 12)

☼ measure and celebrate progress toward your dream (see page 12)

☼ identify roadblocks, and get the help you need to succeed (see page 13)

One of my all-time favorite authors is Dr. Seuss. Several years ago, he wrote a graduation address that found its way into a children's book. If you haven't already read *Oh the Places You'll Go* (or even if you have!), spend a some time with that great philosopher. In parting, let me share a bit of inspiration, Dr. Seuss-style…

"You're off to great places!

You're off and away!

Your mountain is waiting, so get on your way! "

Class List

Teacher: _____   Year: _____

First Name	Last Name	Phone	Birthday	Student #	Parent(s)	Code

The New Teacher's Complete Sourcebook: K–4   Scholastic Professional Books

Kindergarten Information Sheet

Please complete this information and return it to

_____ , Room _____ .

- Child's name: _____
- Child's nickname (if any): _____
- Birth date (month/day/year): _____
- Address (street and zip): _____
- Parent/guardian name(s): _____
- Home phone: _____ Work phone: _____
- Name of person to contact in emergency: _____

  Relationship: _____ Emergency phone: _____
- What language does your child speak at home? _____
- List any health problems your child has: _____

  _____
- List your child's allergies to any foods, animals, or plants: _____

  _____
- List things your child fears: _____

  _____
- List activities your child enjoys doing at home: _____

  _____
- List your child's responsibilities at home: _____

  _____
- List the names and grade levels of your child's brothers or sisters who attend this school:

  _____

  _____
- What else would you like me to know about your child? _____

  _____

  _____

  _____
- What are your expectations for the kindergarten program? _____

  _____

  _____

Student Information

Parent(s): Please fill out and return the following information.

☼ Describe your child's attitude about school in general:

_____

_____

☼ Describe your child's attitude about reading:

_____

_____

☼ Describe your child's attitude about writing:

_____

_____

☼ Describe your child's attitude about math:

_____

_____

☼ List your child's favorite free-time activities:

_____

_____

☼ Describe your child's attitude about his or her brothers and sisters, if any:

_____

_____

☼ Do any of your child's siblings attend this school?
   If so, please list their name(s) and room number(s):

_____

_____

☼ List any special health needs or food allergies your child has:

_____

_____

☼ Is there anything else you would like me to know?

_____

_____

Child's name: _____

Parent/guardian name(s): _____

Full address: _____

Daytime phone: _____ Evening phone: _____

The New Teacher's Complete Sourcebook: K–4 Scholastic Professional Books

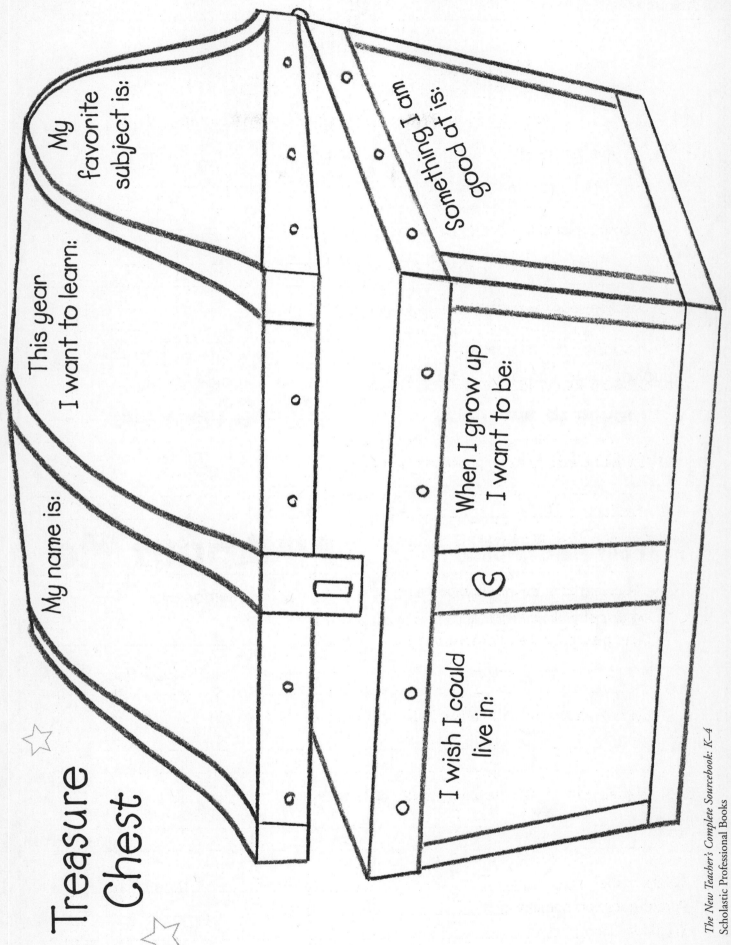

Treasure
Chest

My name is:

This year
I want to learn:

My favorite
subject is:

Something I am
good at is:

When I grow up
I want to be:

I wish I could
live in:

③

About Me at School...

Here is a picture of my favorite thing to do at school.

②

Just About Me...

Here is a picture of my favorite food.

About Me at Home...

Here is a picture of my favorite thing to do at home.

④

All About Me

My name is:

_____

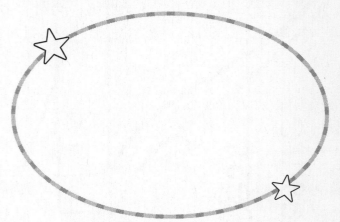

Here is a picture of me!

①

The New Teacher's Complete Sourcebook: K–4 Scholastic Professional Books

Name: _____ Date: _____

Just About Me...

This is how I feel:

⚬ I have lots of friends. _____ yes _____ sometimes _____ no
⚬ I am shy. _____ yes _____ sometimes _____ no
⚬ I am funny. _____ yes _____ sometimes _____ no
⚬ I am brave. _____ yes _____ sometimes _____ no
⚬ I like to daydream. _____ yes _____ sometimes _____ no
⚬ I get along with others. _____ yes _____ sometimes _____ no
⚬ I like to be a leader. _____ yes _____ sometimes _____ no

These are my favorites:

⚬ Animal _____
⚬ Color _____
⚬ Food _____
⚬ Sport _____
⚬ TV Show _____
⚬ Musician _____
⚬ Place to Go _____
⚬ Thing to Do _____

When I grow up I want to be a/an _____

because _____

_____

I like to read about:

_____ adventures   _____ comics   _____ friends
_____ cooking   _____ fantasy   _____ people
_____ drawing & art   _____ mysteries   _____ scary things
_____ history   _____ poetry   _____ sports
_____ places   _____ space   _____ other:
_____ science   _____ cars
_____ animals and insects _____ dinosaurs   _____
                                                     _____

The New Teacher's Complete Sourcebook: K–4 Scholastic Professional Books

Name: _____ Date: _____

About Me at School...

I like doing these things at school:

_____ reading	_____ science	_____ art
_____ math	_____ health	_____ library
_____ computers	_____ music	_____ other:
_____ P.E.	_____ spelling	_____
_____ writing	_____ social studies	_____

☼ I am a good reader.	_____ yes	_____ maybe	_____ no
☼ I am a good writer.	_____ yes	_____ maybe	_____ no
☼ I am good at math.	_____ yes	_____ maybe	_____ no
☼ I am good at science.	_____ yes	_____ maybe	_____ no
☼ I am good at social studies.	_____ yes	_____ maybe	_____ no
☼ I am good at computers.	_____ yes	_____ maybe	_____ no

When I have free time in class, I like to: _____ .

At recess, I like to: _____ .

My best friend at school is: _____ .

I like him/her because: _____ .

☼ I like to read alone.	_____ yes	_____ sometimes	_____ no
☼ I like to read out loud.	_____ yes	_____ sometimes	_____ no
☼ I like to work in groups.	_____ yes	_____ sometimes	_____ no
☼ I do good work.	_____ yes	_____ sometimes	_____ no
☼ I work hard.	_____ yes	_____ sometimes	_____ no
☼ I like to help.	_____ yes	_____ sometimes	_____ no
☼ I like to learn.	_____ yes	_____ sometimes	_____ no
☼ I follow school rules.	_____ yes	_____ sometimes	_____ no

This year, I hope that my teacher will : _____

_____

_____ .

The New Teacher's Complete Sourcebook: K–4 Scholastic Professional Books

Name: _____ Date: _____

About Me at Home...

My family calls me: _____

I have _____ brothers and _____ sisters.

_____ of them go to this school. They are in grade(s) _____.

I have _____ pet(s). It is (They are):_____

_____

_____.

I like to do these things with my family:

_____ build things   _____ games   _____ read

_____ crafts   _____ plays   _____ sports

_____ music   _____ shop   _____ watch TV

_____ sew   _____ trips   _____ other:

_____ talk   _____ computer   _____

_____ cook   _____ movies   _____

When I'm by myself, I like to: _____

_____.

When I'm at home:

☼ I eat healthy foods.	_____ often	_____ sometimes	_____ rarely
☼ I play outside.	_____ often	_____ sometimes	_____ rarely
☼ I read.	_____ often	_____ sometimes	_____ rarely
☼ I watch TV.	_____ often	_____ sometimes	_____ rarely
☼ I talk on the telephone.	_____ often	_____ sometimes	_____ rarely
☼ I have trouble seeing.	_____ often	_____ sometimes	_____ rarely
☼ I have trouble hearing.	_____ often	_____ sometimes	_____ rarely
☼ I feel tired.	_____ often	_____ sometimes	_____ rarely
☼ I get sick.	_____ often	_____ sometimes	_____ rarely
☼ I have allergies.	_____ often	_____ sometimes	_____ rarely

The New Teacher's Complete Sourcebook: K–4   Scholastic Professional Books

Chair
Manager

Song
Leader

Flag
Bearer

Line
Leader

Door
Holder

Host or
Hostess

The New Teacher's Complete Sourcebook: K–4 Scholastic Professional Books

Mail
Person

Messenger

Room
Checker

Teacher's
Assistant

Chooser

Secretary

Pencil Sharpener

Caboose

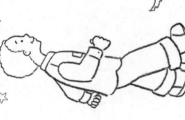

Substitute

Librarian

Historian

Zoo Keeper

176

Sharing

Clean Up

Go Home

Pledge

Snack

Lunch

Computer

Daily
News

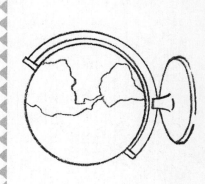

Social
Studies

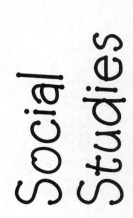

Calendar

Math
Centers

Math

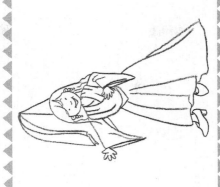

Special Event

Drama

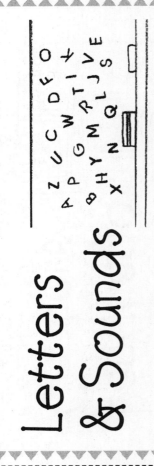

Letters & Sounds

Science

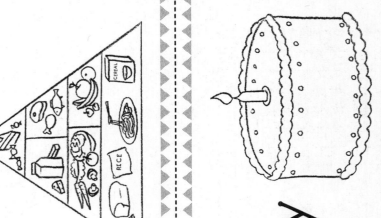

Health

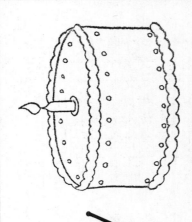

Birthday

Language Centers

Writing Together

Writing Alone

see dog
cat like rain

Words

Reading Together

Reading Alone

The New Teacher's Complete Sourcebook: K–4   Scholastic Professional Books

P. E.

Art

Library

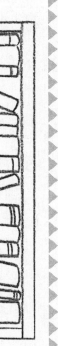

Music

Reward Cards

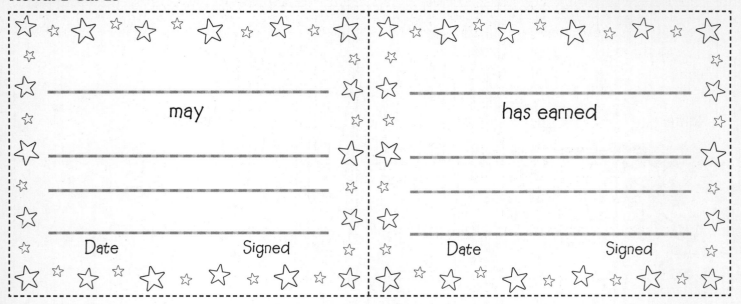

may _____

_____

Date ____ Signed ____

has earned _____

_____

Date ____ Signed ____

Behavior Bucks

One Behavior Buck

One Behavior Buck

One Behavior Buck

One Behavior Buck

"I've Been Caught Being Good" Chance Slips

I've been CAUGHT being good!

I've been CAUGHT being good!

I've been CAUGHT being good!

I've been CAUGHT being good!

The New Teacher's Complete Sourcebook: K–4   Scholastic Professional Books

Weekly Point Card

Name: _____   Comments:

Description	M	T	W	TH	F	Total

Friday Report

Name: _____   Date: _____

Description	Total

Total Points
Possible: 25

Assignments Missed:

Homework Missed:

Comments:

Parent/Guardian Signature: _____

Date: _____

Baseball Behavior Card

Name: _____

Week of: _____

Behavior to Improve: _____

Friday

Thursday

Wednesday

Tuesday

Monday

Comments: _____

_____

Parent/Guardian Signature:

_____

Name: _____

Week of: _____

Behavior to Improve: _____

Friday

Thursday

Wednesday

Tuesday

Monday

Comments: _____

_____

Parent/Guardian Signature:

_____

The New Teacher's Complete Sourcebook: K–4

Scholastic Professional Books

Problem Solving

"Together, we can do it!"

Describe the problem:

☼ Who was involved? _____

☼ What happened? _____

_____

☼ When did it happen? _____

☼ Where did it happen? _____

☼ Why did it happen? _____

_____

How did you feel while you were having the problem? _____

_____

_____

What could you do to solve the problem? _____

_____

_____

What could the teacher do to help you solve the problem? _____

_____

_____

Signature: _____ Date: _____

Progress Report

Teacher: _____

Student: _____ Date: _____

☼ Behavior:

😊 😐 ☹

☼ Participation:

😊 😐 ☹

☼ Skills:

😊 😐 ☹

Progress Report

Teacher: _____

Student: _____ Date: _____

☼ Behavior:

😊 😐 ☹

☼ Participation:

😊 😐 ☹

☼ Skills:

😊 😐 ☹

Progress Report

Teacher: _____

Student: _____ Date: _____

☼ Completes tasks in a timely manner:

😊 😐 ☹

☼ Follows directions:

😊 😐 ☹

☼ Participates in class activities:

😊 😐 ☹

☼ Works well with others:

😊 😐 ☹

Language:

Mathematics:

Comments:

The New Teacher's Complete Sourcebook: K–4 Scholastic Professional Books

Progress Report

Week of: _____

_____ had some problems this week
in the area(s) marked below. Please go over this report with your child and discuss
ways in which any difficulties can be resolved. Sign and return this form on Monday
morning along with any questions or comments you may have.

I appreciate your cooperation. Through our continued efforts, we can help your child
be successful in school.

Thanks!

Behavior

____ Excessive talking

____ Disrupting class

____ Being unkind

____ Fighting

Academics

____ Reading/Writing

____ Math/Computer

____ Science/Health

____ Social Studies

Class Work

____ Missing

____ Incomplete

____ Poorly done

____ Homework

Questions or Comments:

_____

_____

_____

_____

Parent/Guardian Signature:

_____

Progress Report

Week of: _____

_____

had an excellent week!

Your child displayed super behavior, a great attitude, and was prompt in turning in quality work.

It was a pleasure to work with your child this week. Please join me in thanking him/her for his/her efforts and attitude.

A special achievement for this week was:

_____

Thanks,

_____

Conference Notes

Name: _____ Date: _____

Conferencing With: _____

Area(s) of Improvement: _____

_____

Area(s) of Concern: _____

_____

Goal(s): _____

_____

Action(s) to Take: _____

_____

The New Teacher's Complete Sourcebook: K–4   Scholastic Professional Books

Brain-Building Activities for Summer Vacation

(Grades K–2)

Here are some activities for you and your child to explore this summer. Feel free to substitute any activities that would be more appropriate in your situation. It is a good idea to set aside a specific time each day for the explorations so they don't get lost in the shuffle!

MONDAY	TUESDAY	WEDNESDAY	THURSDAY	FRIDAY
Plant a lima bean in a paper cup filled with soil. Begin a learning log for your child to record what happens each day of the week.	Read any children's book together. After reading, make stick puppets of the main characters out of construction paper and popsicle sticks. Put on a puppet play.	Look for places where people use math every day. Talk about the importance of learning to work with numbers.	Have a family meeting to discuss rules and routines for the summer. As a family, decide who is responsible for what and what will happen if the jobs don't get done.	Each Friday, think about the things you did this week. Spend some time making a journal entry for each week by writing or drawing. Start today by decorating your journal.
Boil another lima bean for ten minutes, then plant it. Again, have a learning log to record what happens.	Read any children's book together. After reading, use watercolor paints to create a picture of the book's setting.	Make ten collections of ten things (bottle caps, rubber bands, pencils, beans) and place each set of ten in a zippered baggie. Practice counting, adding, and subtracting with the sets.	Draw a picture of each person in your family. Make a list of the things all members have in common. List things that make you unique in your family.	Don't forget to journal! Also, enlist your child's help in writing the grocery or "to do" list.
Freeze another lima bean for 24 hours, then plant it. Again, have a learning log to record what happens.	Read any children's book together. After reading, fold a large piece of paper in thirds. Draw or write what happened in the beginning, middle, and ending.	Use a pizza or a pie to demonstrate fractions of a whole. Count the number of slices and figure out what fraction is left as each person takes a slice.	Go to the public library to find a book on people from another culture. Read it together and list how they are alike and different from you.	Don't forget to journal! Also, make a list of questions you'd like to ask your friends or each member of your family, then ask them.
Check all three lima beans. Make comparisons of the observations recorded in the learning logs. Discuss good growing conditions for limas.	Read any children's book together. After reading, make a two-column chart labeled "real" and "make-believe." Go through the book again and draw or list items in the correct column.	Use mental math to estimate how many items you have in your grocery cart. Count them together at the checkout counter.	As you're out running errands, talk about the different occupations you see. Discuss what the jobs are and why they are important.	Don't forget to journal! Also, think about the occupations you saw yesterday. How do they use writing in their jobs?
Read *The Empty Pot* by Demi. Enjoy the story, then plant some flowers.	Read any children's book together. After reading, act out the story together.	Do addition and subtraction problems with macaroni, beans, or other objects.	Get a flag and practice the Pledge of Allegiance. Draw a picture of the flag.	Don't forget to journal! Also, write your own pledge to your family.

Brain-Building Activities for Summer Vacation

(Grades 3–4)

Here are some ideas for things to do to keep your brain at its best so you'll be ready for the next school year. Many of these activities require at least one other person. If there isn't an adult around, do the activity with your little brother or sister, or even your old teddy bear!

MONDAY	TUESDAY	WEDNESDAY	THURSDAY	FRIDAY
Discuss ways in which characters from books, TV shows, or movies are alike and different.	Choose an important, useful word to learn to spell each day.	While riding in the car, use mental math to add the numbers on the license plates you see.	Read to discover how waves are set in motion. Make an "Ocean in a Bottle," using blue-colored water and cooking oil in a clear plastic liter bottle.	Have a family meeting to share ideas on new family rules and responsibilities for the summer.
Design your own crossword puzzle or word search.	Write questions for a talk show interview with characters from a book you've read.	When you get up in the morning, figure out how many hours it will be until your favorite TV show starts.	Read about any water insect. Draw it and write a description of it to share with a friend.	If your family is planning a trip this summer, use a map to plan your route and calculate the distance from your home to your destination.
Use the dictionary to look up unknown words from a newspaper article.	Use a tape recorder to record yourself reading a favorite book to share with a younger child. Make the story sound interesting.	Estimate, then measure the distance from your front door to your neighbor's front door. Use a meterstick or yardstick for measuring.	Design a raincoat that people in the future would wear.	Walk around your neighborhood with an adult. Write down the street names and any landmarks. Draw a map of the area.
Alphabetize the family phone list, holiday card list, grocery list, or any other kind of list.	Write and send a letter to get information about an endangered animal or an environmental problem.	Watch a baseball game and determine one player's batting average for that game (number of hits divided by times at bat).	Read to discover the size of raindrops and the speed at which they fall.	Use an atlas to locate and list our 50 states and their capitals. Learn the names and locations of at least 10 Western states.
Predict what will happen next in a book, TV show, or movie.	Turn your favorite comic strip into a paragraph. Make sure to use quotation marks for the dialogue.	Set out an open container of water. Measure the amount and check it daily to find the amount of evaporation. Try other liquids, too.	Build a weather station in your backyard. Compare the data you gather with the TV weather report.	Read the newspaper and cut out articles about the different continents. Sort the articles and save them in a notebook.

Index